SINGLE ISSUES

A **WHOLE-CHURCH** APPROACH TO **SINGLENESS**

STEVE CHILCRAFT
SHEENA GILLIES
RORY KEEGAN

Contents

HOW TO USE THIS BOOK 2

INTRODUCTION As easy as ABC? 3

RESOURCES 7

Session 1 IDENTITY Who am I? 13

Session 2 RELATIONSHIPS Right relating 19

Session 3 SEXUALITY Thanks for the gift? 25

Session 4 SOCIETY What's the world coming to? ... 31

Session 5 CHURCH Have we got it together? 37

Session 6 SERVICE His Majesty's Single Service ... 43

How to Use this Book

Acknowledgments

In November 1987 the Evangelical Alliance held a symposium on singleness. Out of that emerged a process of consultation with church leaders and members to explain the needs of single people in the church. A further outcome was the establishment of EA's Singularly Significant initiative.

A booklet called *Singularly Significant* was published in 1989. It contained resources for group activities and Bible study. It was edited by Veronica Zundel and included contributions by Fran Beckett, Steve Chilcraft, Chris Cook, Martin Hallett, David Hawker, Jenny Joice, Harry Sprange and Heather Wraight. This book has grown out of that original publication.

The writing team is particularly grateful to John Earwicker, Head of Church Life for Evangelical Alliance, for giving permission to adapt and add to material first published by Singularly Significant. (The Singularly Significant initiative came to an end in 1996.)

Thanks are also due for contributions from Steve Tilley and Rose Ayton.

Single Issues **aims to help church leaders think about and address some of the key issues of singleness in today's church. It is designed to be used in a variety of ways:**

- **for personal study**
- **as a leadership team**
- **for house groups and other small groups**
- **as the basis of a six-part course**
- **as a whole-church teaching resource.**

Throughout the book the emphasis is on a whole-church approach to singleness. For this reason many of the activities are planned for groups including both married and single people.

The book contains:

An **INTRODUCTION** offering an up-to-date ABC of singleness.

RESOURCES including notes for two sermons; information about helpful agencies; suggestions for organizing a 'singleness event'.

Six **SESSIONS** focusing the key topics of Identity, Relationships, Sexuality, Society, Church and Service. Each **SESSION** contains:

- An introductory **BRIEFING**.
- Two pages of **GROUP ACTIVITIES** from which leaders can select according to the needs of their groups. Each session features a deliberately provocative **HOT SPOT** discussion starter.
- Two pages of **BIBLE EXPLORATION** followed by suggestions for **ACTION** and **PRAYER**.
- A **PERSONAL PROFILE** of a present-day single person. These interviews may be used to help start discussion; the views expressed in them are, naturally enough, the personal opinions of the interviewees.

INTRODUCTION

As *easy* as ABC?

They've always been there in the church – people without partners. Some are very involved, others less so. Some are happy and well-adjusted, others have problems. Some are making progress in their Christian lives, others are struggling. In short, they're no different from anyone else – apart, that is, from being unpartnered. So if that's the only difference, why the need to explore 'Single Issues'? Here, by way of introduction, are twenty-six possible reasons.

Adding up the evidence A few years ago Evangelical Alliance's *Singularly Significant* network invited a selection of church leaders to make a rough guess of how many single people were in their congregations. Almost without exception they underestimated the number revealed by a subsequent survey. Most had no idea of the reality of the situation. The inquiry revealed that, on average, at least thirty-seven per cent of the adults in a church will be single – that's all kinds of singleness, including people who have never been married, people who are separated or divorced, and widows and widowers. In an urban situation that percentage will probably be higher. And if government statistics are any guide (see page 31), it's a percentage that is likely to keep pace with the expected steep increase in the number of one-person households.

As the new millennium arrives, this diverse people group is going to be making its presence felt in the church – simply by force of numbers, as much as anything else. Already many churches are acknowledging the need to broaden the focus of their ministry. The ongoing support of marriage, family and children will never lessen in importance. But as churches are re-discovering their role as missionary congregations, so the need to develop a genuinely 'whole life' focus becomes unavoidable.

Boxes and boundaries What about encouraging singles' groups within the church? A good idea, or an example of the kind of fragmentation that we should be trying to avoid? If they encourage us to box people into neat categories, then they are probably best avoided. Without meaning to, we can foster a 'grass is greener' attitude which distances married and single people from each other. What really matters is that we all learn to be more open and supportive with one another: being a godly married person brings as many challenges as being an obedient single person.

Community It is a biblical principle that we are born as social animals, we are designed to be in community. Will the late twentieth century win any accolades for its contribution to the development of human community? Probably not. One of its defining features has been the splintering of shared standards, values and attitudes into a narrowly-focused individualism. It's not unfair to suggest that the western church has done little to challenge those attitudes. In fact, in our emphasis on individual spirituality and in our concentration on the nuclear family, we have positively 'bought into' a limiting 'me and mine' mind-set. Being a member of God's new community, the church, is about much more than being part of a nuclear family – it's about servanthood, mutual commitment and redeemed relationships that are based on our new status in Christ. So, for example, what does it say about our attitude to the church if we unthinkingly treat marriage as a 'rite of entry' into adult responsibilities?

In vivid picture language, Jesus described his new community as a banquet with everyone invited. Paul gives us the image of the church as a Body, made of interdependent parts. In that context it's vital that we ensure that people are treated equally on the basis of their identity in Christ and their gifting by God. To think of marriage as the norm and singleness as a deviation from that norm, is as limiting as assuming that God favours one age group over another. We have no mandate for that kind of discrimination.

Divorce Though it may not always get it right, at least the church has centuries of experience to draw on in its support of people who become single when a partner dies. Not so with people who are separated or divorced. Sometimes they can feel that they are being kept at arm's length – the unspoken message is, 'You've failed once – can we trust you?' There will always be a tension between our pastoral concern for individuals and the need to promote God's view of lifelong marriage. But our 'state of society' should encourage us to develop our skills in understanding and supporting people making the traumatic transition from marriage to second-time singleness.

Expectations For some people singleness is a temporary phase. For others it's a lifelong reality. According to age and circumstances, a single Christian will experience a variety of expectations and attitudes from within the church. Something is definitely wrong if we continue to communicate, however unintentionally, the impression that to be unmarried is to be abnormal. The fact that singleness may be a period of transition for some, doesn't mean that it must be for all. In all the biblical teaching on marriage, there's nothing to say that it is the 'rite of passage' into full humanity. So why do so many churches continue to treat single people as if it is?

Families and friendship Equating 'family' with 'nuclear' family is a bit like making a movie entirely composed of close-ups. In the end it's not even helpful for those 'in the frame'. And – much worse – doing so instantly creates a supporting cast of misfits. Broaden the focus, and it's possible to see rich, and largely unexplored ways of relating. What are we doing, as churches, to teach, encourage and support the lost art of friendship? Shouldn't the church, of all places, be a safe, suspicion-free environment in which it's possible to enjoy a wide variety of relationships?

Gay people welcome Some Christian people remain single because they have a homosexual orientation. Their 'discipleship journey' is neither more nor less challenging than that of their heterosexual fellow-believers. Sadly, though, it can be a very lonely one. The emergence of a vocal 'gay lobby' within the church has had at least one positive result: it has broken the silence that led many to assume that homosexuality only exists 'out there'. Specialist ministries and support groups offer valuable help to Christian homosexual people. But real progress in this area depends on the whole church waking up to its responsibilities. That's why it's so important that we broaden our view of family, community and friendship – it *is* possible for a gay Christian to live an obedient life within the church, and a full and satisfying one as well.

Hard questions Every stage and aspect of life brings its share of thorny problems. Whatever the issue, no one should feel, 'I can't say that aloud.' That doesn't mean we have to include intimate issues in every sermon, or to turn house groups into therapy sessions. But it is vitally important to make everybody aware that no issues are 'off limits' and that every question will be listened to, respected and given an honest answer.

Intimacy Anyone can live without sex. No one can live without love. Being a single person needn't mean spending your life in a state of emotional permafrost. The need for intimacy is a basic, God-given human need. Shouldn't the church be the place where we learn, mainly through example, a wide variety of 'right relating'? That means that we should encourage same-sex and cross-sex friendships without putting pressure or hidden agendas onto them. We don't have to make hugging compulsory, but we should acknowledge that everyone has a need for closeness, affirmation and support.

Jesus A biblical approach to singleness has to focus on Jesus and his earthly life. His singleness gave him the opportunity to enter fully into the kind of ministry that he was here on earth to do. His lifestyle was full – and so were his relationships. They were varied and meaningful, cutting across conventional cultural boundaries. He made the most of his freedom and yet valued intimate friendships. He made himself fully available to people, which, of course, has its down as well as its up side.

Key issue The issue of discipleship has to be at the heart of any thinking about singleness. Through his Son, God calls *all* of us to be holy and, through his Spirit, empowers us to be so. Everyone, married or single, needs to be challenged to lead a life 'worthy of the calling' we have received (Ephesians 4:1). And if we're serious about our responsibility to bring everyone to maturity, we'll want to be certain that we don't make marital status a stumbling block for anybody.

Loneliness The common assumption is that all single people are lonely. It *is* a major issue for many, but as the songwriter wrote, 'it ain't necessarily so'. Being smothered with attention is worse than being ignored. What matters is that the church gives everyone the space to develop real friendships. A new believer remarked poignantly, 'I'm glad I've kept my non-Christian friends – people at church are too busy for friendship.'

Modelling This is what used to be called 'setting a good example'. If a church is serious about developing a genuinely inclusive ministry, then the leaders must demonstrate a wholehearted commitment to the nurture and mobilization of single people in the congregation. (One church closed down all its week-night activities for six months with the express intention that everyone – minister included – should work on developing friendships.)

'No win' situation Single people can find themselves in a curious 'double bind'. Outside the church, people think you're strange because you are not having sexual relationships. Inside the church, you're labelled strange because you're not married. Can't win? It can feel like that. Problems can be intensified if, within the church, your singleness is used as a reason for denying you a meaningful role, or for depriving you of responsibility.

Ouch! There's no need to adopt a 'kid gloves' sensitivity towards each other. But it only takes a little thought to avoid many of the remarks that cause toe-curling embarrassment to single people. Here are three classics: after a wedding, 'Your turn next!'; at the end of a visit, 'Do come back one day – with a wife / husband'; at any time, 'Hurry up – you don't want to miss the boat.'

Pressure and postponement Many of us continue to assume that to be half of a couple is to be normal and to be alone is to be somehow less than human. Singleness is a kind of social Colditz, somewhere to be escaped at all costs. Some well-meaning people see their role as a kind of long-distance escape committee, doing everything to aid the single person in his or her perilous journey towards the altar. Such pressure is bad enough – worse is the implied sense of a life postponed. That kindly meant 'Well, maybe one day...' actually says, 'Quite frankly, the person you are *today* isn't good enough.'

Quality of life How you feel about yourself is, in part, the result of how others behave towards you. Say, for example, you are a thirty-something manager in industry. In the workplace your marital status is an irrelevance. What does it do for your self-esteem if, at church, you are being constantly reminded of it? In this context, it's probably true to say that single women fare worse than single men. If your sense of self-worth regularly receives that kind of beating, it's unlikely that your Christian growth and discipleship will flourish.

Responsibility If something is a church issue, then it's a shared issue. We can't all initiate action, but we can all pray and offer encouragement. There's no justification for single people to adopt an 'uptight' attitude, seeing themselves as the victims of an uncaring church. Neither do married people have the right to say, 'Single? That's *your* problem.' If we're in the church, we have to be in it together – 'single issues' are a common responsibility.

Sexuality To be human is to be a sexual being – and it's encouraging that in recent years there's been increased emphasis on the goodness of God's gift of sexuality. But the 'gift metaphor' begs a very big question for single people. 'Thanks very much, *but what do I do with it?*' In a culture which bombards us with sexual images and messages, it's vital that the church offers teaching and support that recognizes the reality of people's daily experience.

Teaching The problem isn't a matter of too much teaching on marriage and not enough on singleness – that kind of thinking compounds the belief that marriage and

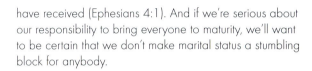

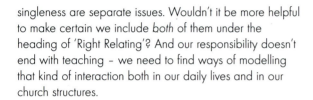

singleness are separate issues. Wouldn't it be more helpful to make certain we include *both* of them under the heading of 'Right Relating'? And our responsibility doesn't end with teaching – we need to find ways of modelling that kind of interaction both in our daily lives and in our church structures.

Understanding Real community begins when people are prepared to make the imaginative leap into sharing another's experience. Some unmarried people seem to sail through life untroubled by being unpartnered. Others may experience a profoundly painful sense of loss, particularly when life's middle years begin. The native American saying holds true for both single and married people: 'If you want to know who I am, walk a mile in my moccasins.'

Virtual singleness There's a unique kind of tension when one spouse is involved in church while leaving his or her non-believing partner at home. For some couples it's a simple matter of 'You do your thing and I'll do mine'. For others, it can cause serious stress. It won't help matters if others at church raise their eyebrows when a person in this situation seems reluctant to join a house group, or to attend yet another meeting.

What? No sex? Living an obedient Christian life is a tough challenge regardless of your marital status. But there's one area in which it's truthful to say that single Christians are at more of a disadvantage than those who are married. Building and sustaining a successful marriage isn't easy – but at least Christian husbands and wives can be encouraged by the fact that our society still broadly believes that fidelity within marriage is 'a good thing'. Any such agreement about the rightness of single people remaining celibate until marriage vanished decades ago. Tell your workmates that you're having trouble in your marriage and they'll probably show sympathy. Try telling them that you're struggling with your commitment to celibacy. Well, you probably won't even try. At best you'll get pity, at worst, ridicule and contempt.

Being a disciple of Jesus Christ is all about adopting a radical lifestyle. Today's 'cultural climate' means that single Christians need particular encouragement and support on this tough-but-true aspect of their calling. It will involve both up-front teaching and ongoing pastoral concern – but it will only be meaningful if all Christians are encouraged to grow in their willingness to be vulnerable to one another.

X-ers Generation X, a popular name for today's twenty-somethings, is a shorthand phrase for the outlook and attitudes of many young people in the nineties. According to the culture watchers, it's typical of 'X-ers' to be suspicious of large organizations (including the church), but to be very positive about small-scale networks. Generation X places a high value on friendship. What are the implications of that for any church wanting to be relevant to today's YSAs (young single adults)?

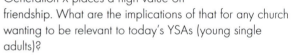

Year 2000 Recent years have witnessed many churches doing some hard thinking about communicating the gospel – and then acting upon those reflections. As a result, new believers *are* coming into our churches – many of them from backgrounds and lifestyles with little or no experience of traditional 'church culture'. We need to be certain about our faith, but we also need to ask ourselves about the relevance of many of the practices, traditions and modes of expression of our week-by-week church life. What better encouragement for some serious spring cleaning than the arrival of a new millennium?

Zest for living Jesus declared, 'I have come that they may have life, and have it to the full' (John 10:10). He promises that fullness, through his Spirit, to *all* believers – young, old, married, single. The church is a place for living life to the full – a good enough reason for 'Single Issues' being on every church's agenda.

RESOURCES

Sermon Notes 1:
SINGLE-MINDED
Matthew 19:12

Aim To help the whole church better understand the place of single people in the church; to help stimulate appropriate action.

Introduction: Singleness today

It is good that most churches stand up, and speak up, for the family. But problems begin when we limit our concerns to the nuclear family of mother, father and dependent children.

Statistics Only one third of the members of most churches consist of people in the 'nuclear family' category.

- 35% of those attending church, aged over 18, are single
- Of these, 68% are female and 32% are male and...
  63% have never married
  13% are separated or divorced
  24% are widowed.

- The numbers of single people in churches broadly reflects the numbers of single people in the community, but the church has more widows and fewer divorcees.

- The number of young single people is growing as people are marrying later. The balance of male to female under the age of thirty is 1.3 women to every man. In society as a whole there is a surplus of single men of marriageable age – a contrast to the situation in most local churches.

(Source: The Evangelical Alliance's survey of British evangelical churches, 1992)

This growing sector of the church has long felt neglected and undervalued.

Assumptions Many believe that marriage is superior to singleness. Is this a Biblical perspective? Or simply a secular view? Are single people second-class citizens? Many feel they're 'on hold' pending their 'elevation' to married status. Should marriage signal their acceptance as mature adults able to take a 'proper' role in the church? Such prejudices contribute to an inappropriate sense of failure.

Family values Is it time to rethink our concept of the church as a family, to be more inclusive of single people? Body of Christ must include and mobilize *all* members. Otherwise, both individuals and whole church lose out. Pastoral issue of mutual responsibility is not main problem: church has suffered because it has neglected gifts of many single people. Traditional roles: single women – baby-sitting and children's work; single men – youth work. Some jobs considered exclusive territory of married couples: pastoral counselling, house group leadership. Anecdote: single Christian leader told by minister: 'Despite your theological training, we can't appoint you as house group leader – you're single.' In that church Elijah, Daniel, Jeremiah, Paul and Jesus would have been disqualified from house group leadership.

Bias Do we show bias ourselves? We need to examine our attitudes and assumptions.

Old Testament perspective

Singleness in ancient Jewish culture God created Adam. Having looked at what he had made, God said that it was 'very good'. To suggest a single person is imperfect or incomplete is to deny the goodness of what God made. (Jesus was the only perfect human – and he

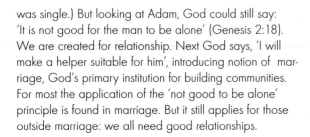

was single.) But looking at Adam, God could still say: 'It is not good for the man to be alone' (Genesis 2:18). We are created for relationship. Next God says, 'I will make a helper suitable for him', introducing notion of marriage, God's primary institution for building communities. For most the application of the 'not good to be alone' principle is found in marriage. But it still applies for those outside marriage: we all need good relationships.

From this passage and God's command, 'Be fruitful and increase in number' (Genesis 1:28), the Jewish rabbis taught it was a sacred duty to marry and multiply. Most males were married by age of twenty; girls were married on reaching child-bearing age. Singleness was virtually unknown. If a man was single it was because something was wrong with him. Thus God's commands to some of the prophets to remain single are significant. Jeremiah was forbidden to marry (Jeremiah 16:2). Ezekiel remained a widower (Ezekiel 24:15-27). Hosea's separation from his wife was a symbol of the broken relationship between God and his people.

New Testament view: a radical alternative

Jesus and singleness Key text: Matthew 19:12. Jesus had been answering a difficult question about divorce. The disciples were amazed at his teaching on faithfulness and the responsibilities of married men: 'If such is the case of a man with his wife, it is better not to marry' (19:10). Jesus follows this with a profound insight into the subject of singleness. A eunuch is a castrated man: his impairment may also be caused congenitally. The Jews abhorred eunuchs, excluding them from priestly service (Leviticus 21:20) and from worshipping in the temple (Deuteronomy 23:1). 'Eunuch' was a term of abuse. Possibly Jesus attracted such abuse because it was so unusual for a normal man of his age to be single. If so, his use of this word is startling. What was seen as derogatory, Jesus turns into an example of virtue.

Three kinds of singleness Jesus uses 'eunuch' as a metaphor for single people. Of his three categories: the first two were recognized by the rabbis as legitimate reasons not to marry; the third was a radical alternative.

1. '(Those) who have been so from birth,' are those who are single for congenital reasons. Few people are in this category. Those with physical disabilities may find it harder to find a suitable partner, but there is no reason why they should not so do. Some recent scientific research suggests the existence of a 'gay gene' which means some people may be born with 'inbuilt' homosexual orientation. If this is true, Jesus' words can apply, by extension, to those who do not marry because of same-sex orientation.

2. '(Those) who have been made eunuchs by others,' are single for circumstantial reasons. Few today suffer castration. However, there are many who are single because of circumstances, not choice. In surveys, up to ninety per cent of single people say they would prefer to be married. Reasons include: 'I've never met right person'; 'My career made marriage difficult'; 'I'd been so hurt I could not trust a man/woman again'; 'I had to look after my elderly parent' and so on. This second group constitutes the large majority of those who are single today.

3. '(Those) who have made themselves eunuchs for the sake of the kingdom of heaven,' are single by choice. Some opt for singleness for a period of time, intending to marry later. A few choose singleness because of other priorities, such as a career or the freedom it brings. These reasons may have nothing to do with Christian faith: the dramatic growth in numbers of single people in the last twenty-five years has little to do with seeking the Kingdom of God. In Biblical terms singleness means celibacy. Today, most young single people expect to be sexually active. One of the great challenges we face in reaching this country for Christ is how we deal with those who are single in the eyes of the law but living as if married.

Others choose lifetime celibacy for the sake of serving God. This teaching of Jesus' was a radically new concept. No longer should his hearers regard marriage and having children as their primary duty, but they should put God first. For some this would mean forsaking marriage. It is a high calling, if a hard one. Many people felt the call of God to serve as overseas missionaries, and went knowing that it might mean losing the chance of marrying. Many single people went in pioneer roles, in dangerous places to take the gospel where it had not been proclaimed. Those who did so were rightly regarded as heroes of the faith. Have we lost respect for those who make similar, if less dramatic, choices today? ('Oh, poor thing. What a shame he/she doesn't have a family.')

Conclusion

Jesus' strong affirmation of singleness needs fresh recognition today. Understanding the diversity of single people is a helpful start. We need the positive view of Scripture to outshine the negative view of singleness we inherit from society and each other. Let's examine whether single people in our church feel 'second-class citizens'. If they do, what we can we do together about it? As we deal with any prejudice in our hearts, whether we are single or married, so we will liberate others to find their rightful place in the Body of Christ.

RESOURCES

Sermon Notes 2: POSITIVELY SINGLE
1 Corinthians 7

Aim To develop a biblical perspective on living a single life.

A customer in a Christian book shop asks: 'Do you have any books on Singleness? There's nothing in the sections on "Family" or "Christian Life".' The assistant replies: 'Try looking in "Counselling".' Singleness is seen as a pathological condition – a 'problem' to be solved.

Singleness and marriage

Singleness is a state parallel to marriage: different, but with contrasting strengths and weaknesses. One in three adults is single – a diverse group of people: socially, and in age, background and experience. Some are 'ever single'. Others have been married, but through reasons of separation, divorce or death now find themselves on their own. Many younger people see singleness as a temporary state. Looking around, it's easy to identify young people, families and elderly people. But you can't identify single people unless you know their circumstances. This diversity means that common issues and needs may be easily overlooked.

Attitudes to singleness

We can't generalize about single people's attitudes towards their singleness: they range from struggle, through reluctant acceptance, to enthusiasm. Two questions asked by many single Christians: 'Am I called to be single?' and 'Do I have the gift of singleness?' Often those who yearn for marriage and family life feel they have no gift for a lifestyle they did not choose or desire. Few single Christians have made a commitment to lifelong celibacy and perceive their singleness as temporary. Do they have the gift of singleness? How should single people view their status?

The spiritual gift of singleness

The only spiritual gift that's less popular is martyrdom! Our society is so good at alleviating pain that we shrink from anything which appears difficult or hurtful. Reluctance to face hard aspects of life and faith means we may lose benefits they bring. Pursuing a pain-free life is an illusion; through pain we may find God and life in its fullness. In a pleasure-orientated society that emphasizes 'personal fulfilment', singleness is bound to get a poor review. Compare this negative attitude with Paul's. At first sight it may seem off-putting, but his mixture of personal testimony with advice to his friends makes a powerful cocktail of wisdom.

A killjoy God?

To many the idea of lifelong celibacy seems as attractive as a cold bath in the Arctic circle. Some mutter stoically through clenched teeth: 'Well, God, your will not mine be done.' But we shouldn't take the perverse view of discipleship: 'If I really want it, it must be wrong'. Life may be tough, but never because God delights in hurting us. He loves us and if he asks something of us that seems beyond our capabilities, he promises the grace to help us cope.

First-century Corinth

Corinth was famous for sexual permissiveness. In first century BC, the temple of Aphrodite was staffed by 1000 female slave-prostitutes. By the first century AD the city was an affluent commercial centre, a market place of conflicting philosophies. Most Corinthians admired the relentless pursuit of personal goals in trade, pleasure and physical development. Others reacted against libertarianism and embraced an ascetic lifestyle, believing that the body was evil: they renounced all pleasures including sex.

The city's culture influenced the young Corinthian church. Some members assumed their new freedom from sin and the law licensed them to do whatever they liked. (In Corinthians 6:16, Paul deals briskly with those defending sex with prostitutes because it 'only' affected the body.) At the opposite extreme, others advocated celibacy for all, teaching that even married couples should refrain from intercourse if they truly wanted to be spiritual (7:2-5). Paul addressed the question of marriage and singleness against these two extreme positions. His teaching is neither anti-sex nor anti-marriage: he urges a balanced view of both. Note also that the church may have faced persecution (7:26). Other factors are Paul's awareness of the shortness of human life, and his belief that the return of Christ may have been imminent (7:29,31).

Paul's teaching

'Stay as you are' (7:8,10,12,26, 40) is Paul's main message for single people considering marriage *and* for married folk seeking a way out of their commitments. He supports the concept of celibacy – but it must be for the right reasons. He states that we have all received gifts from God (7:7). Marriage is a gift – and so is singleness. To live in either state requires God's grace and enabling. Both have positive and negative aspects. Neither is easy, but both are good.

Gifts may be welcomed, developed, ignored or even despised. Many would shun the gift of singleness. It rarely comes as the result of a transforming spiritual experience. Some do receive a lifetime calling to celibacy, but the grace to 'live the calling' is developed over a prolonged time. Whether for a season or a lifetime, it's possible for a man or woman to accept the gift wholeheartedly – and so enjoy its benefits and grasp its opportunities whilst 'modelling' what is a genuinely 'alternative' lifestyle.

Rejecting the gift, even if it's only temporary, isn't good. By focusing solely on marriage, some single people do themselves and the community a disservice. By running away from accepting God's grace to be single, they miss present opportunities for relationships, service, happiness. If they truly want to prepare for marriage, they should make the most of themselves as single people, developing their gifts, skills and relationships in accordance with God's commands.

The advantages of singleness

Paul was probably widowed (or perhaps his Jewish wife had left him after his conversion). From his own experience, he believed that there were many advantages in being single for the sake of the Kingdom of God. These may be summarized as follows.

Freedom from legitimate concerns (7:32a) Then, as now, life was complex: work, family, church, community involvement are all important responsibilities. Singleness simplifies one major area. A married person must give time and effort to pleasing his or her partner and, in many cases, to caring for their children. Some single people may object that things are different today. Full-time work, running a home single-handed, responsibility for elderly relatives plus church commitments can mean they, too, feel overwhelmed. Recognizing this qualification, it's still generally true that singleness simplifies things.

Freedom from stress (7:26) We may not face persecution in the way that the first Christians encountered it, yet there are plenty of trials today. Both single people and married face sickness, unemployment, financial pressures and difficult relationships. It's important to recognize that single living may often be very demanding when one struggles unaided with household problems or illness. Yet, facing some of these issues is often more straightforward if it touches only you, rather than you *and* your dependants.

Freedom to concentrate on priorities (7:29-31) Compared to those with families, most single people have greater flexibility with time, money and energy. Single people may have more freedom than married people to take up some forms of Christian service. Single people are also freer to develop a wide range of relationships. Generally, they have more time for social activities. As with time and money, such freedom can be used selfishly, or generously.

Freedom to please God (7:32b) This is Paul's final and most important assertion. It's not that married people do not have to please God in all they do, but that single people are freer to do so. The key difference Paul states is that a married person has divided priorities: earthly concerns and eternal ones (7:33-34). But the single person may concentrate on pleasing the Lord, without having to consider a partner.

Conclusion

Throughout, Paul is being positive. He stresses that his counsel is not to restrict or deprive but is for the good of the individuals concerned, of the church under pressure, and for the extension of God's Kingdom. His concluding words are significant (7:39-40). A widow has the unquestioned freedom to remarry but he suggests she will be happier if she does not. The sovereign God is at work among us too. For reasons we may not fully understand many of us are single. For so long as he allows any of us to be single we do well to listen to his words to us through Paul. Make the most of singleness. Use its freedom to please God and serve others. It is a great privilege and the whole church must support those who put God first in this way. There *is* a price to be paid, but it is possible to be *positively* single.

RESOURCES

Single Focus:
A PROFILE OF AGENCIES

True Freedom Trust
True Freedom Trust (TfT) was founded in 1977 by Martin Hallett and Canon L Roy Barker. Martin had been involved in a homosexual lifestyle before his Christian conversion and saw the need for more understanding in the church. The majority of people who contact TfT are committed Christians who believe that homosexual relationships are not compatible with Christianity. Many feel unable to talk about their personal struggles. This in itself is a terrible reflection on the quality of fellowship and trust within the church. TfT encourages churches to face this issue. Inevitably the problem of singleness surfaces. The issue of homosexuality is clearly a very important one for the church today and TfT's approach of compassion and understanding which seeks to honour Christ is very important.

TfT maybe contacted at PO Box 3, Upton, Wirral, Merseyside L49 6NY Tel: (0151) 6530773. TfT is a member of the Evangelical Alliance.

CLASP
Christian Link Association of Single Parents (CLASP) is an independent, non-denominational association which provides help and encouragement to all Christian single parents, regardless of how they became single parents.

Individual members have the opportunity of being linked with others in their area. A newsletter is sent to members three times a year. A pen-friend scheme is also in operation. The national organization maintains a link with all members and is willing to be a listening ear, offer information and answer queries where possible. CLASP can also supply speakers to share with others the challenges and blessings of being a single parent.

CLASP may be contacted at Linden, Shorter Avenue, Shenfield, Essex CM15 8RE Tel: (01277) 233848. CLASP is a member of the Evangelical Alliance.

CFF
Christian Friendship Fellowship (CFF) is a nationwide organization which runs activities for single Christians that have a social and spiritual emphasis. CFF has a network of more than 150 local groups; occasionally groups in the same region get together for special events. CFF may be contacted through its central office in Bawtry Hall, Bawtry, Doncaster, South Yorkshire DN10 6JH Tel: (01302) 711007. CFF is a member of the Evangelical Alliance.

CRUSE
Cruse Bereavement Care is a charity founded in 1959. Their help is available to anyone who has lost someone close to him or her through death. Cruse has 190 branches nationally. Contact Cruse at 126 Sheen Road, Richmond, Surrey TW9 1UR Tel: (0181) 9407638. For the Cruse Bereavement Helpline (office hours) call (0181) 332 7227.

RESOURCES

Single Activity:
A SINGLENESS WEEKEND

Single herself, and noticing the growing number of single people in her church, Sarah Allerton was delighted when her minister started to discuss the possibility of a weekend to address singleness issues. She was pleased to join in the planning, working with the church leadership. In an interview with *Single Issues*, she looks back and assesses the success of the initiative.

What are the key issues of singleness in the church?
For me, it's a mix of issues: celebrating freedom *and* facing pain and loss. The pain (spasmodic not chronic) is about felt exclusion and self-esteem: all those sermon illustrations based on family life are often appropriate, but do married clergy realize they can be painful? My raw spot is Mothering Sunday! Which leads on to self-esteem – that nagging irrational feeling that I must be a freak not to be married or have children. But I certainly don't think only singles 'suffer' – I well recognize how un-nurturing some marriages are. I value my singleness because of the freedom it gives me. I also think the costs and benefits of celibacy are not discussed – we are merely exhorted to be good!

Why the need for a Singles' Weekend?
We hoped to legitimize discussion of the issues: to recognize that they are *real* issues, not just private pain. We wanted to encourage a greater sense of common humanity in the church. Whether married or single, life is stressful and we need to be sensitive to each other. And we hoped to allow more honesty and expression of vulnerability without people being 'pathologized'. We hoped to give single people a sense of 'strength from numbers'.

Where did the energy for the project come from?
I guess from pain, and the clergy's experience in pastoral care. For me, it came from the belief that if you face your fears and self-doubt in a supportive environment you can escape the 'victim role'. The minister was very much the promoter of the event. It felt timely; there had been marriage nurture weekends, so this was a logical development.

In your planning and preparation did you have any guiding principles?
We wanted to include formerly married as well as never-married people; to provide evidence of couples valuing single people and to address both homosexuality and heterosexuality. We opened the event to people from other churches – this helped us focus on issues and avoid 'in-house' grumbling.

What shape did the weekend take?
We began with a good dinner on the Friday evening, prepared and served by couples, at which we introduced our two guest leaders. The Saturday was planned as a conference-style day with several main sessions and group discussions. (The themes followed and materials used were similar to many of the ideas and resources to be found in this book.) The aim, which we achieved, was to prepare a list of recommendations to take back to our home churches. On the Sunday, morning and evening services were on the theme of singleness.

What do you think could have been done differently?
The discussion groups might have benefited from a 'facilitator' to summarize, and highlight common threads, give psychological, sociological or theoretical interpretations. People felt good to have been able to share. But I doubt if those troubled by homosexuality felt able to talk openly about their 'secret'.

And what about the impact on the church?
The message that singleness is an important issue was duly given to the whole church, and that felt good in itself. Looking back, we should have reviewed the need for further action after, say, six months or a year.

Session 1: IDENTITY

Who am I?

A sense of identity – of 'being' and 'belonging' – is as vital to health as breathing, eating and sleeping. Living without a sense of identity brings emptiness and fear of rejection. When trying to answer the simple question 'Who am I?' causes confusion, we feel valueless. We are hurting and hurt others, and relationships are hard to maintain.

Our sense of identity begins to be formed in babyhood: the vulnerable, dependent child needs touch, care and affirmation from parents to say, 'You are special and we are thrilled with you.' Insecure parents find it hard to give this unconditional acceptance; as the child grows, they may give the unspoken message, 'You are not good enough.' Later, these negative messages affect relationships with other children. As puberty approaches, the child's developing sexual identity must be affirmed and not undermined.

As Christians we know that our identity is secure because of our Christ-won status as God's adopted children. But because we live in a fallen world, all of us have been damaged in the development of our sense of identity. Often we try to find our 'self-meaning' in someone else – a spouse, a lover, a close friend; or in a cause; or in our job or ministry.

Take your partners

We place a high value on the 'partnered' state; being 'in a relationship' is a sign of being a healthy, happy, acceptable, whole person. Of course, there's nothing wrong with being in a good relationship. Identity problems begin when we start valuing the partnered state at the expense of its alternative.

Is coupledom really the norm for everyone? Does having no ring on the third finger of your left hand make you a misfit? If you aren't one half of a joint bank account or mortgage agreement does that necessarily make you one of life's plucky also-rans? What if you turn up alone at the office Christmas party – does that automatically qualify you for the label 'sad person'? In fact are relationships other than married ones (or ones that lead to marriage) somehow of inferior quality?

In search of self

So perhaps it's not surprising that for single people, the 'search for self' can be more intense, and perhaps more frustrating than for other people. As 'nobody's wife' am I just my parents' daughter? Am I merely a 'sterling church worker'? As a bachelor, am I less of a man than my friends who are married and fathers. Who values me for myself? Only in God can we find our true identity and so relate freely to others.

Half-value?

'Their printed invitation said, "Please bring your other half." I was grateful to have the option of inviting a partner. But the phrase "other half" irritated me. The depressing implication trickled into my consciousness: they don't think I'm a complete person. Never mind my character, my career, or my achievements – as an unpartnered human being I'll never rate more than fifty per cent.'

Group Activities

1. IDENTITY PARADE

Aim To focus on the sources of our sense of identity.

'What's your name and where do you come from?' asks the host of a popular game show. But what do you say to identify yourself after you've given the basics of name and home town? Talk briefly about the ways in which we label ourselves. Invite group members to write up to ten short sentences, each one beginning with the words, 'I am...'. Stress that there are no 'wrong' answers and discourage too much pondering. Assure people that sharing what has been written is entirely optional.

When group members have finished, ask them to mark their lists as follows:

- Place a tick by sentences that are about things you do.
- Put an arrow by sentences that are about your relationship to others.
- Put a plus sign by sentences that make a positive statement.
- Put a minus sign by sentences that make a negative statement.
- Put a cross by sentences connected with your relationship with God.

Invite people to talk about what they have written. Where do we get our sense of identity? What role is played by parents, friends, teachers, employers?

2. INSTANT RESPONSES

Aim To 'sample' a range of responses to singleness.

You will need four large pieces of paper and some coloured pens. Write the following words, one in the centre of each piece: single; married; bachelor; spinster.

Give a pen to each group member. Invite them to write on each paper the words and phrases they associate with the central word: for example, 'bachelor' might elicit 'footloose and fancy-free'. Encourage people not to ponder too heavily: place a five-minute time-limit on the writing part of the activity. Place the sheets where everyone can see them. Discuss the results.

3. CHECK THOSE ATTITUDES

Aim To explore assumptions underlying our sense of identity.

Read the following statements to the group. Discuss the view of identity that each one shows.

- The book includes recipes by Mrs Billy Graham.
- I used to be a keen dancer, but now I'm a Christian.
- The deceased was a pillar of the church.
- I'm only a housewife.
- She's single, but she's very fulfilled.
- He's one of those militant gays.
- Feel free to bring your other half.
- I am loved, therefore I am.

4. SINGLED OUT?

Aim To explore 'gut reactions' to both partnered and unpartnered states of life.

Read this poem by Veronica Zundel to the group. It is based on a thesaurus entry.

Roget's Entry Under 'Married'

Partnered, paired
mated, matched,
wived, husbanded

and handfast, hitched
in double harness

a union, an alliance, a bond, a tie
a door shut with a click
wedlock

leaving such as poor me
(a frayed rope end, unspliced)
outside

unwooed, unasked
unmated, unwed

defined by negatives
half of what never was whole.

Ask the single members of the group (including those who are widowed and divorced) how they respond to the poem. Then ask the married members for their response.

The following questions are for the single members of the group:

- At what age did you first think of yourself as 'single'?
- Would you describe yourself as voluntarily single?
- Or is it something you have found hard to accept?

5. MIND YOUR LANGUAGE!

Aim To explore how our attitudes are expressed in what we say.

'At a Christian family holiday I was leading seminars on singleness. During one worship session the leader said. "All the Mums and Dads sing this verse, and all the children sing the next". I was neither. Suddenly I felt I didn't exist. I sat quietly and didn't sing.'

- Have any members of the group had similar experiences?
- How can things we say unintentionally betray our attitudes to marriage and singleness?
- If it's possible to avoid sexist or 'ageist' remarks, how could we try to avoid attitudes that might be labelled 'couplist' (or 'singlist')?
- What could your own church do to avoid or counteract this kind of incident?

HOT SPOT: Desperation point

Pat said: 'I'm not given to self-pity, but I have experienced the desperateness of being single – something which I feel the church still doesn't take seriously. What I'm thinking of is not just the loneliness but, at times the overwhelming sense of low self-esteem and crisis of identity. There's an ongoing self-questioning: What's wrong with me? Why does that seemingly inadequate person have someone and I, who am less inadequate, don't? What am I doing wrong? When I meet someone do I come on too strong, or not strong enough? And what if I decided to go out with a non-Christian? Why can't I be kissed or held too?'

It's a mistake to assume that all single people are similarly desperate. But it would be complacent to ignore the painful aspects of life for many people in the church.

For discussion, reflection or prayer:
- Can we identify any attitudes that contribute to such a sense of broken identity?
- What can we do to build up the self-esteem of people who may feel their singleness is a sign of failure?
- Do any of our current practices, traditions or activities contribute to this problem?

Bible Exploration

1. IMAGE MATTERS

Read Genesis 1:27-28, 31.
What does this passage say about our identity? How should this affect our view of ourselves?

> So God created man in his own image, in the image of God he created him; male and female he created them. God blessed them and said to them, 'Be fruitful and increase in number; fill the earth and subdue it. Rule over the fish of the sea and the birds of the air and over every living creature that moves on the ground' …God saw all that he had made, and it was very good. And there was evening, and there was morning the sixth day.

Read Genesis 2:18, 22-24.

> The Lord God said, 'It is not good for the man to be alone. I will make a helper suitable for him' … Then the Lord God made a woman from the rib he had taken out of the man, and he brought her to the man. The man said, 'This is now bone of my bones and flesh of my flesh; she shall be called 'woman', for she was taken out of man.' For this reason a man will leave his father and mother and be united to his wife, and they will become one flesh.

Note: 'helper' in 2:18 means 'partner' not 'assistant'; compare how it is used of God in Psalm 30:10.

- What does the passage say about how our identity is linked to other people?
- How important a part do you think our maleness or femaleness is of our identity?
- Are these verses only about marriage, or do they say something to single people too? If so, what?

2. REASONS TO BE SINGLE?

Read Matthew 19:3-12.

> Some Pharisees came to him to test him. They asked, 'Is it lawful for a man to divorce his wife for any and every reason?'
>
> 'Haven't you read,' he replied, 'that at the beginning the Creator "made them male and female", and said, "For this reason a man will leave his father and mother and be united to his wife, and the two will become one flesh"? So they are no longer two, but one. Therefore what God has joined together, let man not separate.'
>
> 'Why then,' they asked, 'did Moses command that a man give his wife a certificate of divorce and send her away?'
>
> Jesus replied, 'Moses permitted you to divorce your wives because your hearts were hard. But it was not this way from the beginning. I tell you that anyone who divorces his wife, except for marital unfaithfulness, and marries another woman commits adultery.' The disciples said to him, 'If this is the situation between a husband and wife, it is better not to marry.' Jesus replied, 'Not everyone can accept this word, but only those to whom it has been given. For some are eunuchs because they were born that way; others were made that way by men; and others have renounced marriage because of the kingdom of heaven. The one who can accept this should accept it.'

- Translating this passage into today's terms, list reasons why people may be single. Which do you think are good reasons?
- In an unfallen world, would everyone be married?
- What do you think of the idea of singleness as a special gift or calling?

Read Matthew 22:23-30.

> That same day the Sadducees, who say there is no resurrection, came to him with a question. 'Teacher,' they said, 'Moses told us that if a man dies without having children, his brother must marry the widow and have children for him. Now there were seven brothers among us. The first one married and died, and since he had no children, he left his wife to his brother. The same thing happened to the second and third brother, right on down to the seventh. Finally, the woman died. Now then, at the resurrection, whose wife will she be of the seven, since all of them were married to her?' Jesus replied, 'You are in error because you do not know the Scriptures or the power of God. At the resurrection people will neither marry nor be given in marriage; they will be like the angels in heaven.

- How did the Sadducees see the woman's identity?
- What is the point of Jesus' answer?
- Does 'no marriage in Heaven' mean 'no deep relationship in Heaven'? What else might it mean? How might it affect us now?

Read Romans 3:21-26; Galatians 3:26-28.

> But now a righteousness from God, apart from law, has been made known, to which the Law and the Prophets testify. This righteousness from God comes through faith in Jesus Christ to all who believe. There is no difference, for all have sinned and fall short of the glory of God, and are justified freely by his grace through the redemption that came by Christ Jesus. God presented him as a sacrifice of atonement, through faith in his blood. He did this to demonstrate his justice, because in his forbearance he had left the sins committed beforehand unpunished – he did it to demonstrate his justice at the present time, so as to be just and the one who justifies those who have faith in Jesus. (Romans 3:21-26.)

> You are all sons of God through faith in Christ Jesus, for all of you who were baptized into Christ have clothed yourselves with Christ. There is neither Jew nor Greek, slave nor free, male nor female, for you are all one in Christ Jesus. (Galatians 3:26-28)

- How does God see us if we are Christians?
- How might this affect our view of our own identity and our marital status?

ACTION

IF YOU ARE SINGLE Think through what your singleness means to you. A problem? An opportunity? A call? A gift?

- Try to hand over to God any feelings of anger, frustration or self-pity. Think of three positive aspects of your life as it is at present. Thank God for them.

IF YOU ARE MARRIED Think through your attitudes to single people. Look out for inappropriate pity or 'stereotyped' views.

- Try to hand over to God any feelings of envy, pity or suspicion. Thank God for the positive aspects of your present state of life. Pray about your relationship with the two or three single people with whom you have the most regular contact.

PRAYER

INTERCESSION Pray for each other – for healing of hurts and fears, and for the development of positive attitudes.

COMMITMENT Re-commit yourselves to each other as God's family.

Personal Profile:
SINGLE AGAIN

Diane and Graham Allen were married in 1974. Six years later, Benjamin was born and Zoe arrived two years after that. Then, in 1986, at the age of thirty-three, Diane died of cancer leaving Graham alone with two children who were then aged five and three. During the next few years, Graham met Alison and they married in 1991. But, just seven months later, Alison died, aged forty-two, from a stroke.

Now, aged forty-three, Graham is an industrial photographer and lives with Benjamin and Zoe who are in their teens. 'They still remember their mother and Alison, of course, but despite missing them both they are accustomed to living with their dad only.

Living with loss

'I was first married in my early twenties – a time when most people are still developing. In that sense, Diane and I grew up together, so consequently not being married now seems unnatural in a way because I believe that the normal state for a person is to be married.'

So what does Graham miss about no longer being married? 'Apart from the sexual part of my life, I miss the companionship and not having anyone to share my life besides the children. It's also having to make decisions: to get into the mental frame of mind where I had to do that alone took a long time.'

However, without dismissing the love he had for both Diane and Alison, Graham recognizes plus points to being single again; 'It has the advantage of not having to compromise myself. For example, in decision making, when you have two people it *is* easier, but the other side to that is that now there's no one to argue with me! To be single is a calling and that is coupled with the fact that God is in control of our circumstances. I'm very conscious of being single but I don't have a great problem with it because that's God's plan for me at this time.'

Attitudes

'People in the church should be treated as individuals, whether married or not. The church doesn't need to do anything except treat people as people. All the church has to do is to be aware that there are special circumstances in being single.'

> '**People in the church should be treated as individuals, whether married or not. The church doesn't need to do anything except treat people as people.**'

For example, single people have less physical contact with others and that is an important area. We're a very tactile family – lots of hugging.'

Graham also warns against illusions about God's will for single people; 'Some single people say, "I think God wants me to be married," – that's a mistake. Also, sometimes people in church see someone who is single and have a "vision" for them and try and impose singleness on them – that's a mistake too.

'People who have never married idealize it: marriage is not necessarily idyllic. Neither is being single. There are blessings and difficulties in both states.'

Session 2: RELATIONSHIPS

Right relating

Jesus had some fairly revolutionary ideas about how human beings should live together. Literally revolutionary: he turned accepted notions of relating upside-down. His order of priorities remains as disturbing today as it was two thousand years ago: to be last is to be first, to be weak is to be strong, you become a servant in order to be a leader, you must die in order to live.

His moral teaching was uncompromising. He preached against sin, but kept company with tax collectors and prostitutes – the apparent contradiction didn't seem to worry him. Again and again, the Gospel writers show Jesus surprising – and shocking – his contemporaries because he chose to 'hang out' with people of whom they didn't approve.

The theme of inclusiveness is at the heart of New Testament teaching about the church. Whether it's in the picture language of a building made of living stones, or of many members making the Body of Christ, the implication is clear: if you're hoping to mix only with like-minded people, then steer clear of the church. Join a social club instead.

No ticket to Utopia

Seemingly irreconcilable differences of race, culture and social status can co-exist within the community of the church. Perhaps this is just a little over-optimistic? St Paul didn't think so. He wrote to his fellow-Christians in multi-ethnic, multi-cultural Colossae, 'Here there is no Greek or Jew, circumcised or uncircumcised, barbarian, Scythian, slave or free, but Christ is all, and is in all' (Colossians 3:11).

This pick-and-mix selection of people had a common bond – their new status as 'God's chosen people'. This mattered more than any other label the world might pin on them. But it didn't guarantee they'd live together in happily-ever-after serenity. Paul was clear-sighted enough to point out the daily demands of life in community. In fact, remembering them was to be as basic and unglamorous as remembering to get dressed each morning: 'clothe yourselves with compassion, kindness, humility, gentleness and patience. Bear with each other and forgive whatever grievances you may have against one another. Forgive as the Lord forgave you' (Colossians 3:12,13).

It's almost two millennia since Paul put down his pen. What about today? One thing seems clear: if there's not something 'distinctively different' about the range and quality of our relationships within the church, then maybe we need to ask some hard questions about what we actually mean when we use the word 'church'.

Breadth and depth

'Welcome to our church family' is a greeting we use often enough. It's a friendly, positive statement. It says that we think of ourselves as more than a collection of individuals. At the same time it's important to remember that nowhere does the New Testament refer to the church as 'family'. The style of living suggested by Paul's use of the word 'household' (Ephesians 2:19) included far more people than we would expect to have living under our roof today. So it's important to use the word 'family' thoughtfully: the broader our definition of community, the more varied will be the range of people who feel at home within it.

Maybe the challenge is to begin by asking God to help us make *everyone* welcome in his church regardless of age, income, background or marital status. God calls all of us into a loving relationship with himself and with one another in a rich variety of contexts: marriage, parenthood, friendship, fellowship. The church should be a place of good, rich, *right* relating – for everybody.

Group Activities

1. GETTING TO KNOW YOU

Aim To learn how our impressions of other people are often based on assumptions rather than factual knowledge.

We often make huge assumptions about each other based on what is really a fairly superficial relationship. How well do we *really* know each other? What are individuals' likes/dislikes, skills/abilities?

Taking a real interest in people is the best way to demonstrate our affection and concern for them.

Each group member needs a paper listing likes and dislikes, skills and abilities together with columns entitled GUESS and REALITY.

Ask group members to get into smaller groups of about six (and not less than four) people. Ask them to choose people they don't know particularly well. Each individual then fills in the 'guess' column for the others in the group. When these are complete, they should consult the rest of the group in order to fill in the 'reality' column and share their results with each other.

- Did the activity provoke any 'I never knew *that*!' discoveries?
- What are the key ways we can ensure that people know we are interested and concerned in their lives 'beyond church'?

2. TRUST

Aim To explore the importance of trust in relationships.

Invite group members to work in pairs for the first part of this activity.

- Think back to an incident which made you realize that somebody could not always be trusted. How did you feel? How significant was it? What were the issues for you then? What are the issues for you now?
- Think of a person you can really trust. What makes this relationship special? Share this with a partner.

Re-group to discuss how trust can be built and maintained between individuals. How do we make ourselves trustworthy?

For a more active alternative, set up an obstacle course in the room. Invite people to choose a partner. One of each pair volunteers to be blindfolded. The 'sighted' partner then has to guide his or her colleague through the obstacles by spoken instructions.

	GUESS	REALITY
SPEAKS FLUENTLY A LANGUAGE OTHER THAN ENGLISH		
IS AFRAID OF HEIGHTS		
LIKES CATS		
IS AN ONLY CHILD		
READS NOVELS BY TERRY PRATCHETT AND / OR JILLY COOPER		
HATES GARDENING		
IS ADDICTED TO A 'SOAP'		
RIDES A BIKE REGULARLY		
ENJOYS OPERA AND / OR FOOTBALL		
CAN PLAY A MUSICAL INSTRUMENT		

3. POWER

Aim To explore the role of power in our relationships in the church.

Churches are often seen by those outside them (and sometimes within them) as authoritarian and powerful institutions. Is this impression in any way true with regard to your own church?

- Think of a time when your own will (and possibly feelings) were over-ridden by someone in a more powerful position than your own – at work or at church? How did that make you feel?

How can we ensure that our relationships inside and outside the church show clearly that each individual is valued, listened to and respected?

4. HOLDING HANDS

Aim To discuss the importance of touch in relationships.

Our attitudes to the expression of friendship and affection vary according to our background, age and culture. What's appropriate behaviour at one age, is totally inappropriate at another. What is acceptable behaviour in one part of the world, will be frowned on in another. What factors determine our attitudes – our sense of right and wrong, our 'cultural conditioning', or maybe a mixture of both of them?

- Photocopy and enlarge the drawing so that all group members can see it clearly. Alternatively copy it onto an OHP acetate and project it onto a wall or screen.
- Ask group members to get into pairs. Begin by asking each pair to make up a very brief story to accompany the picture. After a few minutes invite each pair to share their story with the group.
- Discuss the differences between the stories.
- Go back into pairs. Tell the group that the hands are those of two adult males. Once again, invite each pair to provide a short scenario.
- After a few minutes, re-group and listen to one another's stories. What are the differences between them? Do they give us any clues about our attitudes to same-sex friendship?

HOT SPOT: Give us a break!

Joe said: 'In my experience there's nil teaching about the state of going out with someone. You can get away with going out with someone for about six months before people in the church start asking when you are going to get engaged. If that pressure isn't bad enough, another important issue is how you cope (and what can others do) when breaking up with someone? That can be devastating and often full of hurt. Breaking up is hard to do.'

For discussion, reflection or prayer:
- How seriously does our church take the need for teaching on relationships? Do we leave that kind of thing to the Youth Group?
- What practical steps can we take as individuals to encourage the development of good relationships?
- What practical steps can we take as a church to encourage the development of good relationships?
- Have we ever experienced the pressure of 'inappropriate expectations'? Or have we been guilty of applying it?

Bible Exploration

1. GROWING UP

Read Luke 2:41-52.

> Every year his parents went to Jerusalem for the Feast of the Passover. When he was twelve years old, they went up to the Feast, according to the custom. After the Feast was over, while his parents were returning home, the boy Jesus stayed behind in Jerusalem, but they were unaware of it. Thinking he was in their company, they travelled on for a day. Then they began looking for him among their relatives and friends. When they did not find him, they went back to Jerusalem to look for him. After three days they found him in the temple courts, sitting among the teachers, listening to them and asking them questions. Everyone who heard him was amazed at his understanding and his answers. When his parents saw him, they were astonished. His mother said to him, 'Son, why have you treated us like this? Your father and I have been anxiously searching for you.'
>
> 'Why were you searching for me?' he asked. 'Didn't you know I had to be in my Father's house?' But they did not understand what he was saying to them.
>
> Then he went down to Nazareth with them and was obedient to them. But his mother treasured all these things in her heart. And Jesus grew in wisdom and stature, and in favour with God and men.

Also Matthew 4:12-13; Mark 3:20-21, 31-35.

- What does Jesus' growing up tell us about adulthood and relationships?
- Growing up is often described as a journey from dependence to independence: does Jesus' story confirm this or give us an alternative?
- What do the passages tell us about how family life and community life fit together?
- Ask parents in the group to share briefly how they feel about their children growing up and separating from them.
- Then ask single people in the group to share how they feel about their own separating from parents (single parents may wish to speak on both sides).

2. RIVER DEEP, MOUNTAIN HIGH

Read 1 Samuel 18:1-4; 20:41-42.

> After David had finished talking with Saul, Jonathan became one in spirit with David, and he loved him as himself. From that day Saul kept David with him and did not let him return to his father's house. And Jonathan made a covenant with David because he loved him as himself. Jonathan took off the robe he was wearing and gave it to David, along with his tunic, and even his sword, his bow and his belt. (1 Samuel 18:1-4)
>
> After the boy had gone, David got up from the south side [of the stone] and bowed down before Jonathan three times, with his face to the ground. Then they kissed each other and wept together – but David wept the most. Jonathan said to David, 'Go in peace, for we have sworn friendship with each other in the name of the Lord, saying, 'The Lord is witness between you and me, and between your descendants and my descendants for ever.' Then David left, and Jonathan went back to the town. (1 Samuel 20:41-42)

Also You may want to look at Ruth 1:6-18.

- Does our society today still allow for this depth of friendship?
- Does our church encourage it? Should it?

22

3. A PERFECT FRIEND?

Read John 11:1-5,33-35.

> Now a man named Lazarus was sick. He was from Bethany, the village of Mary and her sister Martha. This Mary, whose brother Lazarus now lay sick, was the same one who poured perfume on the Lord and wiped his feet with her hair. So the sisters sent word to Jesus, 'Lord, the one you love is sick.'
>
> When he heard this, Jesus said, 'This sickness will not end in death. No, it is for God's glory so that God's Son may be glorified through it.' Jesus loved Martha and her sister and Lazarus. (John 11:1-5)
>
> When Jesus saw her weeping, and the Jews who had come along with her also weeping, he was deeply moved in spirit and troubled. 'Where have you laid him?' he asked.
>
> 'Come and see, Lord,' they replied.
>
> Jesus wept.
>
> Then the Jews said, 'See how he loved him!' (John 11:33-35)

Also John 12:1-3; 13:1,21-25,34; 15:10-15; 19:25-27; 20:10-16; 21:15-17.

- List all the ways in which Jesus treats his friends in these verses. What impression does John's Gospel give us of Jesus' relationships?
- How do our own relationships compare with this?

ACTION

As a group, list one or two ways you can work for the following aims.
- Providing good models of relationships to growing children, especially children of single parents;
- Promoting greater depth of relationships among single people (not just with other single people!);
- Providing emotional support for the formerly married, both divorced / separated and widowed people and those who have 'broken up';
- Helping single and married people think through issues of singleness and sexuality.

PRAYER

The wires are holding hands around the holes;
To avoid breaking the ring, they hold tight the neighbouring wrist,
And it's thus that with holes they make a fence.

Lord, there are lots of holes in my life.
There are some in the lives of my neighbours.
But if you wish we shall hold hands
We shall hold very tight
And together we shall make a fine roll of fence to adorn Paradise.

Michael Quoist, *Prayers of Life*, Gill & Macmillan (Reproduced by permission)

Personal Profile:
EVER SINGLE

'Like a good sherry, I'm mature, sweet and full-bodied whereas my peer group are into sleeping tablets and bed socks.' Having trained as a psychiatric social worker, Dorothy Guyatt worked in the fields of family therapy and youth work before retiring a few years ago through difficulties which still affect her.

She is also a psychotherapist and is involved in a counselling service at her home. In addition she is the lay chair of a Deanery Synod and a Diocesan Reader. Dorothy's extensive church experience is also marked by the fact she was brought up in the Open Brethren, then became an Anglican, and went over to Rome before finally returning to Canterbury.

Who needs a goldfish?

'I made a definite choice in my late twenties that I would be prepared to stay single. It's lovely and there's a sense of glory and delight. It's true: I'm not conning you with a jolly story – although I do know what it's like to be alone. If someone wants help, I'm free to give it. It's wonderful to work in harness with the Lord without the responsibilities of husband, children and a goldfish.'

Dorothy, who prefers to describe herself as 'ever-single' rather than 'never married', also said, I'm celibate and it's been all right – I do agonize for friends who are tormented because they're not married. Hormones and urges are God-given, after all. I'm a non-practising heterosexual!

'I've always had men friends and it's all been platonic: I've felt that this was God's affirmation of my decision. I enjoy and need male company and they say my friendship is good because I'm not on the hunt.'

Mixed messages

Having once been told by a minister that because she was single, she was a 'non-person', Dorothy is all too aware of the difficulties some single people face. 'The church has no idea how to deal with single people. If you're a single woman you're expected to work in the crèche, run the Sunday School and have problems. Until the church gets this right, there will be more promiscuity because other opportunities to be appreciated and valued don't readily occur. Discussion about sexuality and singleness is never considered and is always repressed in an untidy way. I am frightened by the mixed message that the church gives to single people and that is not helping us to realize the enormous fulfilment available.'.

> **'I am frightened by the mixed message that the church gives to single people.'**

But it's not all the church's fault, she said: 'We don't have to be martyrs to our singleness. Some people are quite uptight about being single, live life through gritted teeth and have an element of bitterness. They throw themselves into inappropriate roles and they never "play": there's no counter-balance. Yet, really if they were joyous and flamboyant that would be a much better advertisement.'

Dorothy believes that 'singles' groups are not the way forward: 'Groups should be generic. I'm not happy about specialist groups according to sex and marital status. I've constantly avoided them.'

No discrimination

So, what is the way ahead for the church? 'I think it's a question of acceptance. Single people are not there to look after others. They need to be involved in things – and not just because they're on their own. There should be no discrimination: the church should treat single people as equals. Individual hospitality is particularly important: as long as they're not asked to come and look after the visiting aged relative.'

'I've thought of trying dating agencies,' Dorothy joked. But, as with all good humour, her punch line was devastatingly on target: 'If people are that desperate to meet someone then the church is failing.'

Session 3: SEXUALITY

Thanks for the gift?

Sexuality is a bit like a fingerprint: basic, unique and absolutely personal. It's a gift from God and it's fundamental to our sense of identity. You can speculate about your own, but you can't make assumptions about anyone else's.

As Christians we believe that, along with every other aspect of our humanity, our sexuality is marked by the consequences of our fallen state. Hence the fact that our experience of it is an infinitely varied mixture of joy and sorrow. If the church is committed to a whole-life focus, issues connected with sexuality have to be on its agenda. Let's explore some of them with the aid of a few more analogies.

Sexuality is like a movie star

Even superstars sometimes suffer from an 'image problem'. It's the same with the Christian view of sexuality. The biblical 'big picture' of sex and sexual relationships is powerfully positive. The complementarity of the sexes, the life-long 'one flesh' relationship between husband and wife, mutual responsibility for God's creation, and some frank endorsements of passionate sensuality – all of these are important features of the biblical version of 'the joy of sex'. But sometimes it seems as if the church is so busy saying what's wrong about sex that it has no spare energy to say what's right.

- Are we communicating a fully-rounded view of sexuality in our teaching and pastoral agendas?

Sexuality is like a holiday brochure

If marriage was a vacation destination, what spot on the globe would it be? Ask around within the church. Possibly somewhere sunny? The Bahamas, perhaps? OK, so there's the ever-present possibility of a tropical storm, but a touch of danger adds spice to life. Despite the fact that the married state doesn't get a very good press, it's still many people's dream destination.

And what if singleness was a destination? In particular, what if Christian 'no-sex-please-we're-celibate' singleness was a destination? Judging from the way many people talk about it, probably nowhere so alluring. Siberia, perhaps? In travel-trade terms, singleness is a 'niche market' requiring specialist promotion for a very discerning clientele.

A joke? Of course. Home, hearth and marriage bed conjure up images of warmth and security – and rightly so. But should we assume that marriage must therefore be the right destination for *everyone*? Are we right to tie a second-class label on other destinations? Is celibacy really the equivalent of a life sentence in a deep freeze?

- Wonderful as married, sexual love may be, are there other ways in which people can grow in godly, loving relationships? After all, anyone can live without sex – nobody can live without love.

Sexuality is like a Gold Card

Sexuality is like a major-name charge card. And a freely-given, Gold Card at that. And we're grateful, very grateful indeed to our heavenly benefactor for his tremendous generosity. Sexuality is a truly wonderful gift. Our gratitude is underscored by the fact that, given the chance, few of us would choose to be sexless beings. But for single people there's more than a little puzzlement mixed in with the gratitude: 'Thanks for the gift, but what do I do with it?'

The problem is that, for us, the card comes with conditions: 'use only in the marriage megastore'. (Try explaining that to your neighbours or workmates – don't expect them to say, 'That'll do nicely.') So when it seems as if everyone except you is out at the January sales, the single Christian adult could do with a little encouragement.

- Are we creating 'safe spaces' within our churches where people can find support and encouragement not only with sexual issues, but with a variety of life's pressure points?

Group Activities

1. 'OOH LA LA!' OR 'OOH LE LE'?

Aim To explore our views on 'appropriate' male and female roles.

As anyone who has ever struggled to learn French will know, the language assigns genders to every noun in the language. What if we were to do the same?

Copy and distribute the following lists of everyday words. Ask group members to decide which ones should be labelled M for masculine and which should be labelled F for feminine. Try to go for 'gut reactions' and, if possible, be guided more by your sense of popular assumptions than by any awareness of contemporary 'political correctness'.

Jobs	**Things**
Bank manager	Spanner
Dancer	Mixer
Nurse	Silk
Inventor	Car
Doctor	Dynamite
Nursery teacher	Needle

Activities	**Concepts**
Ballet	Peace
Opera	War
Rugby	Co-operation
Mountaineering	Aggression
Talking	Nurture
Inventing	Building

Collect the lists and, without revealing sources, count up the 'scores' for the items on each list. What do the results tell us about our attitudes?

2. WHAT, HOW, WHEN AND WHERE?

Aim To introduce pastoral issues related to sexuality.

A group of single and married Christian adults might include the following topics in the 'hot potato' category of a discussion on human sexuality:

> sexual fantasies
> celibacy
> loneliness
> appropriate boundaries with persons of the opposite (or same) sex
> need for intimacy
> same-sex attraction
> masturbation
> memories of past sexual experience
> sexual abuse
> trans-sexualism
> pornography

- Are there any topics that you, as a group, would want to add to the list (or remove from it)? (You may want to do this by distributing slips of paper for people to make anonymous contributions.)
- How can a church community address such issues – through teaching, one-to-one counselling or through promoting its network of small groups? Working in pairs place the items on your list of 'hot potatoes' under the following headings:

> whole-church teaching
> one-to-one counselling
> small groups
> personal friendship
> other

- Can you think of any ways in which your church could move forward in its ability to address these and similar issues?
- To what extent should a church community be unshockable on matters of human sexuality?

3. STRAIGHT TO THE POINT?

Aim To discuss church-based issues related to homosexuality.

Read the following case study.

John and Anthony are both in their early thirties. They have recently started attending St Matthew's and took part in a recent Alpha course. They work locally and live at the same address. Several people in the fellowship assume that John and Anthony are a 'gay couple' and approach the church's leaders to ask what they are 'going to do about them'.

As a group discuss what advice you would give to the leadership at St Matthew's. You may want to consider the following suggestions:

- Do nothing.
- Include preaching on homosexuality in a forthcoming sermon series.
- Suggest to John and Anthony that they may feel more at home elsewhere.
- Check that the basics of biblical teaching on all human sexuality have been covered recently in whole-church preaching and in house groups.

HOT SPOT: 'I had no idea...'

Jill said: 'I became a Christian a few years ago at the age of twenty-six. I had never been promiscuous, but I had been in two serious, long-term relationships. Sadly, the first one didn't work out and, after a very lonely couple of years, John and I met and "clicked". We moved in together some six months before I came to faith. Up to that point I thought that I'd been living a responsible, sensible adult life. When it dawned on me that I was expected to adopt a celibate lifestyle, it came as a very painful surprise...'

Broadly speaking, both church and 'world' agree that fidelity within marriage is a 'good thing'. There's no longer any such agreement on the belief that unmarried people should be celibate.

For discussion, reflection and prayer:

- Is a celibate lifestyle any more difficult today than it was in the past?
- 'The church's attitude to celibacy and single people seems to be, "Grit your teeth and get on with it."' Is that fair comment?
- How can we balance truthfulness with sensitivity in our teaching on celibacy?
- What attitudes need to change in order to encourage single people in this aspect of Christian obedience?
- How 'up front' should we be about celibacy when asked questions about our faith by non-Christian friends?

Bible Exploration

1. CELEBRATING SEXUALITY

Read Song of Songs 2:3-7; 4:10-14.

> Like an apple tree among the trees of the forest is my lover among the young men. I delight to sit in his shade, and his fruit is sweet to my taste. He has taken me to the banquet hall, and his banner over me is love. Strengthen me with raisins, refresh me with apples, for I am faint with love. His left arm is under my head, and his right arm embraces me. Daughters of Jerusalem, I charge you by the gazelles and by the does of the field: Do not arouse or awaken love until it so desires. (Song of Songs 2:3-7)
>
> How delightful is your love, my sister, my bride! How much more pleasing is your love than wine, and the fragrance of your perfume than any spice! Your lips drop sweetness as the honeycomb, my bride; milk and honey are under your tongue. The fragrance of your garments is like that of Lebanon. You are a garden locked up, my sister, my bride; you are a spring enclosed, a sealed fountain. Your plants are an orchard of pomegranates with choice fruits, with henna and nard, nard and saffron, calamus and cinnamon, with every kind of incense tree, with myrrh and aloes and all the finest spices. (Song of Songs 4:10-14)

Write the following question on a large sheet of paper, or on an OHP slide: What is sex for?

As a group, list as many answers as you can think of.
- Look again at the Bible passages and see if you can find support for your views in them.
- Do these Bible passages describe a 'no-holds-barred' attitude to sex or is there an element of self-discipline in them?
- Ask the single members of the group how they react to reading these passages. Then ask the married members.

2. HOT POTATOES

Read 1 Corinthians 6:18-20; 7:1-3,8-9.

> Flee from sexual immorality. All other sins a man commits are outside his body, but he who sins sexually sins against his own body. Do you not know that your body is a temple of the Holy Spirit, who is in you, whom you have received from God? You are not your own; you were bought at a price. Therefore honour God with your body. (1 Corinthians 6:18-20)
>
> Now for the matters you wrote about: It is good for a man not to marry. But since there is so much immorality, each man should have his own wife, and each woman her own husband. The husband should fulfil his marital duty to his wife, and likewise the wife to her husband. (1 Corinthians 7:1-3)
>
> Now to the unmarried and the widows I say: It is good for them to stay unmarried, as I am. But if they cannot control themselves, they should marry, for it is better to marry than to burn with passion. (1 Corinthians 7:8-9)

Try to arrive at a group definition of 'sexual immorality'.
- Most Christians believe sex outside marriage is wrong. List as many reasons for this belief as you can. Which reasons are good ones?
- Which are bad?
- What principles do you think should guide physical involvement between single people?
- What positive things does sexuality give us?
- How can single people enjoy their sexuality rather than seeing it as a burden?

3. RADICAL ALTERNATIVE?

Read 1 Corinthians 6:9-20.

> Do you not know that the wicked will not inherit the kingdom of God? Do not be deceived: Neither the sexually immoral nor idolaters nor adulterers nor male prostitutes nor homosexual offenders nor thieves nor the greedy nor drunkards nor slanderers nor swindlers will inherit the kingdom of God. And that is what some of you were. But you were washed, you were sanctified, you were justified in the name of the Lord Jesus Christ and by the Spirit of our God.
>
> 'Everything is permissible for me' – but not everything is beneficial. 'Everything is permissible for me' – but I will not be mastered by anything. 'Food for the stomach and the stomach for food' – but God will destroy them both. The body is not meant for sexual immorality, but for the Lord, and the Lord for the body. By his power God raised the Lord from the dead, and he will raise us also. Do you not know that your bodies are members of Christ himself? Shall I then take the members of Christ and unite them with a prostitute? Never! Do you not know that he who unites himself with a prostitute is one with her in body? For it is said, 'The two will become one flesh.' But he who unites himself with the Lord is one with him in spirit.
>
> Flee from sexual immorality. All other sins a man commits are outside his body, but he who sins sexually sins against his own body. Do you not know that your body is a temple of the Holy Spirit, who is in you, whom you have received from God? You are not your own; you were bought at a price. Therefore honour God with your body.

ACTION

Use the results of Group Activity 2 ('What, how, when and where?') to start preparing a list of suggestions, recommendations, or simply topics for discussion, that you can pass on to your church leadership team at the end of these sessions.

PRAYER

MEDITATE on Psalm 139:1-18

PRAISE God for creating us male and female – and for the complementarity of the sexes.

THANK God for the aspects of our sexuality that reflect his creativity, strength and compassion.

ASK God for a deeper understanding of our sexuality, and a more profound reliance upon him in order to become the men and women he intends us to be.

- What are the basic truths underlying Paul's advice on sexual behaviour?
- Does the Bible see sexual sin as worse than other kinds? Is there a different standard for men than for women?
- Christian singles are under many pressures in our society. In what ways do we help/hinder them in coping?

Personal Profile: SINGLED OUT

'A good hug never did anyone any harm. It's a great thing when a straight man who knows I'm gay hugs me – it's confirming of his unconditional love for me.' The knowledge that he was loved by God and his friends regardless of his sexuality was a turning point in Graham Alldus's acceptance of the fact he is gay. 'I didn't want to be gay, I'd always struggled with my sexuality and orientation but didn't come to terms with it until a year ago.'

Graham is twenty-seven years old and a student at Bible college. Low self-esteem in his teenage years and the fact he never had a girlfriend in those formative times affected him greatly. 'I wanted to be "normal", to fit in and to be married with children. There was a great social pressure to be so.'

He became a Christian four years ago and soon afterwards undertook counselling about his sexuality. 'It was the best thing for me at that time and helped pinpoint elements of my sexuality. For the next two years I went on asexually and then thought God had sent the right woman – but I realized I wasn't sexually attracted to her.'

No conditions

In September 1995, Graham started at Bible college. 'I went to college to get away from God! I was trying to face up to the question, How can I be gay and a Christian? But within a month God opened my eyes with a profound revelation that he loved me unconditionally regardless of my sexuality. Here was me struggling with my sexuality and wanting to get away from church and everyone else and worrying about what people would think if they knew I was gay. Now, the vast majority of my friends accept me and love me as I am.'

But Graham finds it's not a trouble-free path. 'Before I "came out", people in church and family kept asking if I had a girlfriend. Now, that's changed to, "How can we pray for your healing?"

'My singleness is not just because of my sexuality and sexuality isn't the same as sex. I adhere to a celibacy theology and even before I became a Christian, homosexual activity was not acceptable to me. From my reading of the Bible, I don't condone practice.'

'Before I "came out", people in church and family kept asking if I had a girlfriend. Now, that's changed to, "How can we pray for your healing?"'

Friends

Speaking on attitudes towards single people in general, Graham commented: 'People in church consider that to be normal is to be married, and then if you're married and don't have kids then that's not normal either. My heterosexual friends struggle more with being single than I do, but very often single people make a cross for their own back, like sitting in the back row at church or waiting for someone to phone.

'Close friendships with both single and married people are very important to a single person, homosexual or not. If a person is single because of sexuality and they're not "out", then there may also be a fear of it remaining a secret. Once it's brought out into the light, God can use it. I've found that talking to others helps them to think about the issues.

Hard knots

'The church has to face the issues and accept that gay and lesbian relationships exist. But it's so inextricably entwined to the rights and wrongs of homosexuality and there's often no distinction between identity and practice. Until we tackle the seeming contradiction of being gay and being a Christian, there can be no progress.

'There are so many routes into homosexuality and there are different ways out. I never rule out the possibility that I may end up married with kids.'

Session 4: SOCIETY

What's the world coming to?

In June 1994 the population of the United Kingdom was 58.4 million. The male population was 28.6 million and the female was 29.8 million. Let's look at some other statistics drawn from the government's *1994 General Household Survey* (Office of Population, Censuses and Surveys) and *Social Trends 1996* and *Social Trends 1997* (Central Statistical Survey).

- The proportion of adults aged sixteen and over who lived alone increased from nine per cent in 1973 to fifteen per cent in 1994.
- More than a quarter of households in Great Britain in 1994/95 consisted of one person living alone, almost double the proportion in 1961.
- 'Single Britain will be the reality. By 2016 there will be almost twenty-four million households in England, twenty-three per cent more than in 1991, and more than one in three will consist of people living on their own.' *The Independent,* January 1997 (Source: *Social Trends 1997*, The Stationery Office)
- The proportion of families headed by a lone parent increased from nearly eight per cent in 1971 to twenty-three per cent in 1994.
- In 1994 one in five mothers with dependent children was a lone mother.
- The UK now has the highest divorce rate in the European Community. In 1993 there were 3.1 divorces per 1000 of population. Forecasters expect that this proportion will almost double in the three decades to 2020. (*Social Trends 1997*)

Face the facts

Like it or not, our world is changing. Traditional patterns of family and community life have altered massively in the last quarter of this century. 'Live-alones', single parents, divorced men and women, widowed people: the statistics give the basic details of what is going to be an increasingly insistent challenge to the church. How can we ensure that our church life is attractive and meaningful to people who live outside our traditional definitions of family living?

Changing expectations

Most parents continue to expect that their children will marry; most will probably worry if a son or daughter is still single by the time he or she reaches thirty.

In the past 'single' meant 'celibate' (at least that was the expectation for women) without sexual experience or activity. Nowadays 'young, free and single' has very different overtones.

Courtship patterns have changed, with more freedom for both sexes, and for women to take the initiative in relationships. The days when living together was seen as a daring experiment are long past. And though cohabiting has increased, it remains a prelude to eventual marriage for most couples.

In comparison to twenty years ago, more people are prepared to accept homosexual relationships. It's also true to say that people who profess tolerance may tacitly add: 'As long as it's not my brother / sister / son / daughter.' And, sadly, it's still probably true to say that most Christians with a homosexual orientation are reluctant to 'come out' to more than a very few trusted friends. Consequently they continue smiling through clenched teeth as yet another well-meaning person inquires, 'Still not found Miss or Mr Right?'

In the Asian community, marriage is a parental or community responsibility, and singleness almost unknown. In the British black community, though the older generation is strict and conservative, couples will often not marry until their first child is born. Both these minority cultures have begun to influence thinking in society as a whole.

Amidst all this, Christians struggle to relate to the world and still maintain biblical standards of morality.

Group Activities

1. NETWORKING

Aim To gain an overview of our contacts with single people.

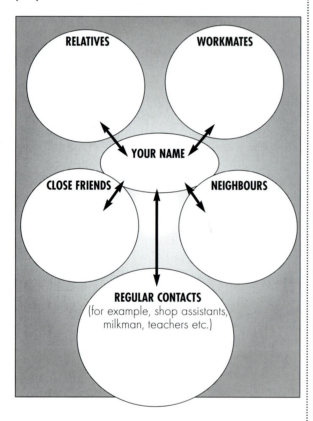

Make copies of the diagram and distribute to group members. Invite them to write on it the names of people with whom they have close contact.

- How many of the people listed are single? How many are non-Christians? (Ask group members to do this without conferring with one another.)
- Compare the results gained by married people and single people in the group.
- Between you, how many single people could you be reaching out to?

2. PEOPLE AND PRESSURE POINTS

Copy the diagram on the facing page onto an OHP acetate. You may also wish to make copies to distribute to group members.

- Using the information given, discuss what you think may be the practical, emotional, social, and spiritual needs of the people listed.
- Which of these does your church already cater for to some extent? Which might it think about providing for more appropriately?
- What recommendations might you want to make to your church leadership team as a result of this activity?

HOT SPOT: *Labelled for life?*

Ben said: 'I'm a parent. I'm divorced and I have recently become a Christian. So much of the church's teaching on marriage and family life leaves me with a massive sense of personal failure. Many church activities confront me with my 'less-than-perfect' status and what first seems like friendliness can easily veer into a patronizing attitude. I'm willing to take my share of the blame for the failure of my marriage. I believe that God has forgiven me – I wish I felt that the church has done the same. The feeling I get is that divorce labels me 'second-class' as a parent, and as a person.'

For discussion, reflection and prayer:
- Being compassionate or being patronizing – what are the characteristics of both attitudes?
- How can we balance endorsement of lifelong marriage with support and encouragement for people whose marriages have broken down?
- What are the key messages that Ben, and people like him, need to hear from the church?

People and pressure points

NAME	Jackie	Jo	Jack	Jim	Jeff	Jenny
AGE	54	38	29	76	48	19
STATUS	Single	Divorced	Single	Widower	Divorced	Single
BASICS	Works in professional Christian ministry; cares for frail elderly father.	Teacher; mother of John (13) and Jessie (8).	Health professional; lives alone.	Retired council worker; lives alone.	Engineer; father of three daughters with whom he has lost touch.	Student; has a 'serious' relationship with fellow-student Jake.
THINGS TO AVOID						
PERSONAL PRESSURES						
POTENTIAL						

Bible Exploration

1. CHECK THOSE ATTITUDES

Read I Corinthians 7:1-16.

Corinth was a very permissive city in which divorce was common. Some Corinthians over-reacted and saw sex as unholy and singleness as preferable to marriage. (It's worth pointing out that 'It is good for a man not to marry' may be Paul's personal view; but equally he may be quoting a view held in Corinth and expressed in 'the matters that you wrote about'.)

> Now for the matters you wrote about: It is good for a man not to marry. But since there is so much immorality, each man should have his own wife, and each woman her own husband. The husband should fulfil his marital duty to his wife, and likewise the wife to her husband. The wife's body does not belong to her alone but also to her husband. In the same way, the husband's body does not belong to him alone but also to his wife. Do not deprive each other except by mutual consent and for a time, so that you may devote yourselves to prayer. Then come together again so that Satan will not tempt you because of your lack of self-control. I say this as a concession, not as a command. I wish that all men were as I am. But each man has his own gift from God; one has this gift, another has that.
>
> Now to the unmarried and the widows I say: It is good for them to stay unmarried, as I am. But if they cannot control themselves, they should marry, for it is better to marry than to burn with passion.
>
> To the married I give this command (not I, but the Lord): A wife must not separate from her husband. But if she does, she must remain unmarried or else be reconciled to her husband. And a husband must not divorce his wife.
>
> To the rest I say this (I, not the Lord): If any brother has a wife who is not a believer and she is willing to live with him, he must not divorce her. And if a woman has a husband who is not a believer and he is willing to live with her, she must not divorce him. For the unbelieving husband has been sanctified through his wife, and the unbelieving wife has been sanctified through her believing husband. Otherwise your children would be unclean, but as it is, they are holy.
>
> But if the unbeliever leaves, let him do so. A believing man or woman is not bound in such circumstances; God has called us to live in peace. How do you know, wife, whether you will save your husband? Or, how do you know, husband, whether you will save your wife?

As a group, list all the differences you can find between Paul's attitudes and today's common attitudes to:
- marriage
- divorce
- singleness.

- How far do you find yourself in sympathy with Paul? What difficulties do you find in accepting his views?
- When thinking about this passage do your emotions and thoughts agree with each other?
- How far does Paul adapt his teaching to the Corinthian culture? How far does he stand against it?
- What guidance does this give us for our society?

2. WOMEN ALONE

Read Acts 6:1-4; James 1:27; 1 Timothy 5:3-10,16.

> In those days when the number of disciples was increasing, the Grecian Jews among them complained against the Hebraic Jews because their widows were being overlooked in the daily distribution of food. So the Twelve gathered all the disciples together and said, 'It would not be right for us to neglect the ministry of the word of God in order to wait on tables. Brothers, choose seven men from among you who are known to be full of the Spirit and wisdom. We will turn this responsibility over to them and will give our attention to prayer and the ministry of the word.' (Acts 6:1-4)

> *Religion that God our Father accepts as pure and faultless is this: to look after orphans and widows in their distress and to keep oneself from being polluted by the world.* (James 1:27)
>
> *Give proper recognition to those widows who are really in need. But if a widow has children or grandchildren, these should learn first of all to put their religion into practice by caring for their own family and so repaying their parents and grandparents, for this is pleasing to God. The widow who is really in need and left all alone puts her hope in God and continues night and day to pray and to ask God for help. But the widow who lives for pleasure is dead even while she lives. Give the people these instructions, too, so that no one may be open to blame. If anyone does not provide for his relatives, and especially for his immediate family, he has denied the faith and is worse than an unbeliever.*
>
> *No widow may be put on the list of widows unless she is over sixty, has been faithful to her husband, and is well known for her good deeds, such as bringing up children, showing hospitality, washing the feet of the saints, helping those in trouble and devoting herself to all kinds of good deeds.* (1 Timothy 5:3-10)
>
> *If any woman who is a believer has widows in her family, she should help them and not let the church be burdened with them, so that the church can help those widows who are really in need.* (1 Timothy 5:16)

ACTION

To do alone:
REVIEW the names on the list made while doing this session's first activity, 'Networking'. Are there any people among them who would appreciate a visit, an invitation to coffee or simply some friendly concern? Decide what action would be appropriate.

To do as a group:
CONSIDER supporting an agency that works with single, homeless adults.

PRAYER

Make a collection of newspaper headlines which draw attention to some of the problems of loneliness and isolation in our society. Use them as the starting point for a time of reflection and intercession.

Women alone in biblical times had little means of support. Christian widows could no longer count on help from non-Christian families.

- What groups in our society do you think have equivalent needs to the New Testament widows?
- What can this passage tell us about our concern for people 'on the margins'?
- Should more support for such people be organized, or is it up to their families?

Personal Profile: SINGLE TRACK

'I've never found relationships easy. I'm always a bit like a train going downhill – and usually there's a crash.' Aged thirty-three, Julie-Ann Hilton is a PhD student in theology, an actress and the mother of eight-year-old Jamal. **'I've never been married and I only have myself and my child to think about. Making decisions can be to some extent easier – there's no one to comment.'**

Julie-Ann and Jamal live in a two-bedroomed, housing association flat with no garden. 'I'd now find it very difficult to live with somebody – not least because of the lack of space. The hard thing for Jamal is that he doesn't have any brothers or sisters with whom he could find company. Isolation is a big issue all round.'

Need for a network

This lone existence presents practical problems: 'I have found solidarity with other women on their own with children, but the hardest thing is finding the right people to act as a network. For example, with childminding, I can study while he's at school but the problem is when I have acting commitments and have to be away overnight or back late. That's hard because obviously Jamal doesn't relate to others as well as he does to me.'

Attitudes

Julie-Ann became a Christian in 1988 when she was still involved with Jamal's father and she was shocked to discover the church's attitude towards her continuing relationship. 'I never realized it was sinful. I became very cynical about the process of relationships between men and women and couldn't accept that men were actually prepared to wait for marriage before having sex.'

Options

She admits to having continued difficulties with the church line on sex, marriage and singleness. 'My experience of being single in the church has been quite an isolating one. I feel the church's general attitude is that people meet someone and get married – and if you don't, you're a little odd and eventually perceived as too old. But for some people, marriage is not something that ever became possible, for whatever reason.

> **'My experience of being single in the church has been quite an isolating one. I feel the church's general attitude is that people meet someone and get married – and if you don't, you're a little odd and eventually perceived as too old.'**

'There are two options: either you remain within the church structure that insists on no sex before marriage or you go to a church that doesn't and understands that that happens. If Jamal's father came back today, I'd want a full relationship with him.'

Julie-Ann's train is going full steam ahead down a single track. 'For now, I'm at the stage of "If you're happy being single and celibate that's good". I like not having anyone interfering with my life and causing me heartache.'

Session 5: CHURCH

Have we got it together?

Too often in the church, single people are viewed as a problem to be solved – or to be suffered. Attitudes can veer between the optimistic ('Quick, find a partner for her') and the resigned ('Too bad he never married').

The tendency to assume that an unmarried person must be a 'potential pastoral problem' can lead subtly to what one observer describes as 'the pathologizing of single people' – surely the very worst kind of labelling.

At other times, it's assumed that single people form a pool of readily available labour ('They're sure to have time.'). Combine the pressure to marry with the push to take on more responsibility and it's not surprising that, for some single people, the church can seem a source of oppression rather than of liberation.

Different folks...

Every church is different and every member – married, single, child or pensioner – will experience church differently. The church community that some single people find open and encouraging may be a place of restriction to others. Also, it has to be admitted that problems may be greater or lesser according to the personalities and attitudes that we bring with us to church.

And, of course, as with all sensitive issues, the topic of singleness brings a definite risk of 'double jeopardy'. As some church leaders know to their cost, it can sometimes seem very hard to win: plan something that's slanted towards single people and you can be accused of being patronizing; fail to plan such an event and you're told you're 'ignoring the issue'.

Being real

So have we got it together? Are 'single issues' a specific area to be addressed, or simply one aspect of our need to re-discover the true meaning of being church? Is it a matter of radical re-adjustment, or more one of redressing the imbalance caused by our tendency to over-emphasize the importance of the nuclear family?

Perhaps it's simply a matter of being real; of being willing to be open and, possibly, vulnerable to one another. Paul's advice to his fellow-believers in Galatia wasn't exactly complicated: 'Carry each other's burdens, and in this way you will fulfil the law of Christ' (Galatians 6:2). Living in obedience to Christ is a challenge for *every* believer regardless of age, sex or marital status.

Plus and minus

So single people may well have a lot to celebrate: many may have more time and money to plough into God's work, and greater mobility for overseas or travelling ministry than would be possible for their married friends. Single adults can be a valuable example to teenagers of how to live a self-controlled, yet fulfilled, life in the world.

And yet, in many churches, a single person could examine the amount of teaching, support and encouragement provided for married people and ask, quite justifiably, 'What about me?' Coping with celibacy, the need for intimacy, loneliness, sexuality – the prickly issues of a solo lifestyle – remain largely ignored. There is a pressing need to discover together what it really means to be the family of God.

Group Activities

1. SINGLENESS AUDIT

Aim To consider the 'single dimensions' of your own congregation.

- If possible, list all the single adults (over 16) in your church. Include all ages and all forms of singleness.
- Now add those who are 'single at church' because their partner does not attend. What proportion of the congregation is this?
- List how many single people are involved in some kind of leadership or teaching role in your church, as: house group leaders; children's work leaders; deacons; PCC / Church council members; youth leaders; workers in church agencies and departments; elders; church school governors; missionaries.
- To what extent are single people represented among your leaders?
- How could the information gathered in this activity benefit your church leadership team?

2. GOING FORWARD TOGETHER

Aim To focus thinking on practical recommendations to church leaders.

Make several enlarged copies of the Evangelical Alliance's Consultation on Singleness (opposite). Cut out each of the recommendations. Invite group members to arrange them in what they feel should be order of priority. If necessary write your own statements to cover areas you feel have been missed. (The list printed here is given in its original order.) Try to come to a common agreement on your 'top ten' recommendations to take to your own church leaders. If possible encourage those in leadership to agree to review, after six months, whether any of the recommendations have been implemented.

HOT SPOT

Wendy says: 'Bob and I have been married for seven years and have two young children. Four years ago I became a Christian. I've really enjoyed my new friendships and fellowship at church. But Bob resents my involvement. How much time should I give to the church, and how much to my husband and kids? The minister's very keen that as many people as possible should go on the church weekend – but it would mean two nights away from home.

'I worry about the mixed messages we're giving to the children. Last year my mother died. She was a lovely Christian woman and I explained to the children about her going to heaven – later Bob gave them a very different slant. So much of church life revolves around attending meetings and I feel guilty I can't go to many. When I suggest a baby-sitter, Bob doesn't often agree. His parents will baby-sit if we want to go out to the cinema, but when I invited him to a church Christmas meal (and he actually said yes!) they suddenly found they were too busy to help.'

For discussion, reflection and prayer:
- What are the main pressures of being 'virtually single' when you come to church?
- How should the church be supporting Wendy, and people in similar situations?
- What should Wendy do about the church weekend?

38

Consultation on Singleness

Late in the 1980s, the Evangelical Alliance surveyed attitudes to singleness in churches throughout the United Kingdom. As a result of those findings, they published the following recommendations.

In all the following recommendations we recognize the responsibility of single people to contribute to all aspects of church life.

The Church needs to develop a theology of singlness within the context of a biblical understanding of relationships within the Kingdom.

We need to recognize the calling of single people to take their equal place within local and national church leadership.

By teaching, example and support those working with youth should present celibacy as a positive and fulfilling way of life.

We need to recover a biblical emphasis on the spiritual gift of celibacy and find positive ways of presenting this to the Church and the world.

Opportunities for exploring alternative models of community living should be provided. Economic pressure, particularly for younger single people, against this must be tackled, e.g. through new methods of housing provision.

Churches should aim to foster a depth of relationship among their members and avoid either isolating single people or pressurizing them into marriage. This may include what some understand as 'covenant' commitment.

Churches should be encouraged to give a greater level of practical pastoral support to single people going through major changes in their lives, and those caring for adult dependants.

There is a need for retirement preparation appropriate for single people and positive channelling of their gifts into a continuing ministry.

Churches should recognize and involve themselves in the changing housing needs of elderly single people.

Churches should actively seek to integrate single parents, separated, divorced and widowed people into the church community, e.g. through hospitality, corporate social activities, shared discipleship groups.

Churches should take every opportunity to grow in awareness of the practical needs of single parents and their children and give appropriate support, e.g. through child care, house maintenance, family link schemes.

Churches should seek through prayer and counselling to provide for emotional healing for those whose identity and relationships have suffered damage.

Churches should establish relevant evangelistic structures directed towards the needs of single people and give active support to those engaged in evangelism and care amongst them.

Forums within churches should be created for single and married people together to discuss personal issues of sexuality.

Radical rethinking is required of the concept and practice of 'family' services.

Preachers should remember that their congregations include people leading single lifestyles.

In church decision-making and government greater consideration should be given to the perspective of the whole range of single members of the congregation.

Increased efforts should be made to recognize, develop and direct the gifts of all single people.

Shared holidays between married couples and single people could be encouraged.

Existing pastoral structures should be assessed and restructured as necessary in the light of the needs of single people.

Bible Exploration

1. BODY MATTERS

Read 1 Corinthians 12:4-7,12-14,21-26.

> There are different kinds of gifts, but the same Spirit. There are different kinds of service, but the same Lord. There are different kinds of working, but the same God works all of them in all men. Now to each one the manifestation of the Spirit is given for the common good. (1 Corinthians 12:4-7)
>
> The body is a unit, though it is made up of many parts; and though all its parts are many, they form one body. So it is with Christ. For we were all baptized by one Spirit into one body — whether Jews or Greeks, slave or free — and we were all given the one Spirit to drink. Now the body is not made up of one part but of many. (1 Corinthians 12:12-14)
>
> The eye cannot say to the hand, 'I don't need you!' And the head cannot say to the feet, 'I don't need you!' On the contrary, those parts of the body that seem to be weaker are indispensable, and the parts that we think are less honourable we treat with special honour. And the parts that are unpresentable are treated with special modesty, while our presentable parts need no special treatment. But God has combined the members of the body and has given greater honour to the parts that lacked it, so that there should be no division in the body, but that its parts should have equal concern for each other. If one part suffers, every part suffers with it; if one part is honoured, every part rejoices with it. (1 Corinthians 12:21-26)

- What are the main things we learn from the picture of the church as a 'body'?
- How does this apply to people with the 'gifts' of singleness and marriage in the church?
- Does your church value married and single people equally, or do you give more attention to one than the other?
- Read Ephesians 2:19; Galatians 6:10; Hebrews 2:11 (NIV). What is meant when the term 'family' or 'household' of God is used of the church? Compare this with the way the term 'family' is used in your church.
- If your church holds a 'Family Service' are there some people who tend to avoid it? Why?

2. TAKING A LEAD

Read Isaiah 8:3; Ezekiel 24:15-19; Jeremiah 16:1-4.

Among the major prophets, Isaiah was married, Ezekiel was widowed and Jeremiah was told not to marry. Hosea suffered marriage breakdown as a sign to the people. (Hosea 1:2-3; 3:1-3.)

Read 1 Corinthians 7:7; 9:5, 15a; Acts 16:13-15; 18:26.

> I wish that all men were as I am. But each man has his own gift from God; one has this gift, another has that. (1 Corinthians 7:7)
>
> Don't we have the right to take a believing wife along with us, as do the other apostles and the Lord's brothers and Cephas? (1 Corinthians 9:5)
>
> But I have not used any of these rights... (1 Corinthians 9:15)
>
> On the Sabbath we went outside the city gate to the river, where we expected to find a place of prayer. We sat down and began to speak to the women who had gathered there. One of those listening was a woman named Lydia, a dealer in purple cloth from the city of Thyatira, who was a worshipper of God. The Lord opened her heart to respond to Paul's message. When she and the members of her household were baptized, she invited us to her home. 'If you consider me a believer in the Lord,' she said, 'come and stay at my house.' And she persuaded us. (Acts 16:13-15)
>
> He began to speak boldly in the synagogue. When Priscilla and Aquila heard him, they invited him to their home and explained to him the way of God more adequately. (Acts 18:26)

40

- Some early church leaders were single, some married, some perhaps widowed.
- In a culture where most people married, why did God select some leaders to be single or to lose their spouse? What messages might this carry?
- What message do you think single leaders might have for today's church?
- What do we learn from Jesus' example as a single leader?

ACTION

To do together:
The following suggestions are for consideration in conjunction with the second of this session's Group Activities, 'Going forward together'.

- Using any information about single people in your neighbourhood which you have gathered (see 'Networking' on page 32) begin to work out a strategy for your church's work and evangelism among them.
- If much of your church work is done by single people, resolve to ask a married person next time a church job needs doing. If some jobs are never done by single people, ask a single person next time.
- Consider setting up a 'singleness advisory group'. Members might include a single parent, an ever-single person, an elderly person living alone, a younger bereaved person. How could such a group help the church?
- Next time you are planning a family service, church social or holiday, check that the interests of single people are on the agenda.

PRAYER

CONFESSION Think of a time when you have made false assumptions about another person. Bring that to God.

THANKSGIVING Thank God for the practical gifts of both single and married people within the church.

INTERCESSION Pray for single workers and leaders in your church, or in the wider church. Pray for any single mission workers known to your group.

Personal Profile:
SINGLE MINDED

'I've enjoyed the benefits of being single, like working irregular hours and travelling, being able to take risks and make spontaneous decisions.' Calvin Portbury puts his experience down to being an independent person from an early age and very much an individual thinker. Aged twenty-nine, Calvin is from Zimbabwe and came to the United Kingdom in September 1996 to spend a year doing voluntary work.

Calvin's single-mindedness also has other benefits: 'I have often been able to stand my ground when pressures of being single have arisen. The pressures have never really bothered me but I recognize that being single is a difficult issue for many people I have met.'

And it's not always been easy for Calvin: 'There are aspects of being single that I have had to work through and still have to. Several relationships I have been involved in have collapsed, largely due to the feeling I was too independent.

Deep needs

'One of my saddest moments was where a girlfriend I really cherished expressed feelings of insecurity because of my sense of independence and said she felt I didn't need her or anyone else. I felt hurt and deeply fragile at that and also helpless since I couldn't find a way of changing it.

'My need for true intimacy, exclusive companionship and the deep fulfilment of such a sharing lifestyle keep growing.'

African view

Having observed attitudes in both the UK and in Zimbabwe, where singleness is not a subject which gets a lot of attention from the church, Calvin said: 'In Zimbabwean churches, single women in their late twenties, especially those with a child from a previous relationship, are under some pressure and fall under suspicion. But there's not much pressure on the guys.

> **'**Some common frustrations are the lack of space, openness and confidentiality in which to talk through personal difficulties about singleness.**'**

Listening

'Looking at the way marriage is held in the nineties it would seem that a lot of people prefer the single lifestyle. From my observation and conversations with others, I feel single people would like and greatly appreciate a confidential listener and to be able to seek real meaning for their personal questions about being single. Some common frustrations are the lack of space, openness and confidentiality in which to talk through personal difficulties about singleness. That's particularly true when singleness is linked to employment insecurity, and where gender roles and status are being redefined in society.

'The church ought to be in the lead on such difficult issues – but often it's been indifferent.'

Session 6: SERVICE

His Majesty's Single Service

There is a long and honourable tradition of single people who have given their lives to serve their Lord in preference to the norm of marriage and family life. Starting with the first followers of Jesus, the church has been deeply indebted to those for whom putting the Kingdom of God first has meant remaining single.

The New Testament writers did not think it important to record whether people were married or single unless their marital status affected their work, as in the case of Peter, James and some of the other apostles (1 Corinthians 9:5) We know that Paul chose to remain single because it made him a more effective servant of Christ (1 Corinthians 7:8,32,35).

In the early church the role of the single person in leadership became increasingly common. In the third century AD, Jerome taught that celibacy was superior to marriage. Ambrose (AD 339-397) believed marriage disqualified a man from ordination. In AD 691, the Eastern Church agreed its policy, which is still the rule today, that those already married could enter the priesthood, although they could not become bishops. A serving priest was not allowed to marry. The Western Church, despite inconsistencies, took a stronger line which insisted that all clergy should be celibate.

Male, mature and married

After the reformation, celibacy was still highly esteemed, but was made optional. Within a short period, Protestants reversed the previous practice and elevated marriage as the preferred status for ministers. This became the norm. Without intending to do so, the Protestant churches came to regard married clergy as superior to those who were single. Ministerial vacancies are regularly advertised with a presumption or stipulation that all applicants be married. However, junior posts such as curacies and youth workers are open to single people. Regardless of character, temperament, gifts or experience, single people are presumed to be less mature than their married counterparts.

Single-minded service

Single people were prominent in the great missionary expansion of the nineteenth century. Henry Martyn (1781-1812) famously declared, 'My love must wait', as he put the task of translating the Scriptures into Hindi, Persian and Arabic before marriage to his beloved Lydia. Single women later came to prominence and became the backbone of many mission fields. Mary Slessor from Aberdeen went to Nigeria's Calabar coast, Amy Carmichael to southern India and Gladys Aylward to China.

Prominent single Christians today include John Stott, Sir Cliff Richard, Dave Pope, Helen Roseveare, Mother Teresa and Simon Hughes MP. All have determined that, for them, marriage was not their priority in life. Others, such as Joni Earickson and Jackie Pullinger, found prominence as single people through their Christian ministries although they married later.

Finding a place

Paul himself is an interesting case. As a leading Pharisee he would have been married, yet at the time he wrote his letter to the Corinthians he was single. There are two suggestions. He may have been a widower or his wife, who would probably have been a devoted Jewish believer, rejected him following his conversion. If the latter scenario is true, it adds poignancy to his comments to believers with unbelieving spouses (1 Corinthians 7:12-14). He may have been through the same painful experience himself.

Single people of all types can find their particular place in God's service. This session will seek to evaluate Paul's reasons for remaining single in the context of modern life and suggest ways that individuals can more fully use their gifts for the benefit of God's kingdom.

Group Activities

1. PROS AND CONS

Aim To take an objective look at the benefits of being single alongside the disadvantages.

Make copies of the grid on the facing page and distribute to the group. Allow people some personal time to start filling in the boxes. Using an OHP acetate with the grid copied onto it, invite the group to brainstorm in order to make a shared list. The suggestions needn't all be desperately serious, so welcome light-hearted comments as well as profound ones.

- Discuss the themes and topics that emerge, some of which may be very personal and others matters of opinion.
- Do married members of the group have different ideas from those who are single?

2. HAND PRINT

Aim To identify and affirm each others' gifts and abilities.

This activity is designed for groups of six people and works best when there's a strong element of trust and mutual respect among them.

- Give each member of the group a plain sheet of paper. Invite everybody to trace around their own hand (fingers splayed) and write their name in the middle of the palm. Now ask them to pass their drawing to their neighbour, who then writes (in one of the fingers) something they have observed that's a positive characteristic or a God-given ability of the hand's owner.
- Pass the sheets on until they return to their owners with comments in all the digits. You may then want to invite members to read aloud the comments they have received.
- If there's time encourage group members to make suggestions of how one anothers' gifts might best be used and developed.

3. ROLE MODELS

Aim To discuss individuals who demonstrate a positive response to singleness.

- Which single people, in Scripture, history or of your own acquaintance, other than Jesus, do you most admire and why?

HOT SPOT

Bill said: 'Assuming trains and buses co-operate, I'm usually home from work on Mondays by 7.00 p.m. That gives me an hour to change, listen to The Archers and cook a meal before heading off to the church council meeting at 8.00 p.m. I'm also involved with the youth group and I play in the music group on Sunday. The minister recently asked me to help with a forthcoming Alpha course: "I know you're busy, Bill, but being single means you have more time than a married person, doesn't it?" Yes, I thought – and my shirts iron themselves, the supermarket delivers my shopping and my lawn recently became self-mowing. Where does this idea come from – that I sail through life on an ocean of free time? Perhaps the minister could suggest when I may find some surplus time to fix the car, re-paint the front door and develop my social life.'

For discussion, reflection and prayer:
- Fair comment from Bill, or does he have a chip on his shoulder?
- How can we avoid making assumptions about the time demands on other people – both married and single?
- It's easy to take other people for granted. Is there anyone in your church, among your workmates or in your immediate family who may be feeling unappreciated at the moment? What could you do to give that person a boost?

Singleness – pros and cons

	ADVANTAGES	DISADVANTAGES
SPIRITUAL		
EMOTIONAL AND SOCIAL		
PHYSICAL AND PRACTICAL		

Bible Exploration

1. BACK TO BASICS

Read Matthew 6:33; Romans 12:1-2; Philippians 1:21.

> *Seek first his kingdom and his righteousness, and all these things will be given to you as well.*
> (Matthew 6:33)
>
> *Therefore, I urge you, brothers, in view of God's mercy, to offer your bodies as living sacrifices, holy and pleasing to God – this is your spiritual act of worship. Do not conform any longer to the pattern of this world, but be transformed by the renewing of your mind. Then you will be able to test and approve what God's will is – his good, pleasing and perfect will.*
> (Romans 12:1-2)
>
> *For to me, to live is Christ and to die is gain.*
> (Philippians 1:21)

These verses offer basic principles for all who seek to follow Christ.

- What are the major elements of discipleship common to all regardless of their marital status?
- Are there any areas that are different for single people?

2. HERE AND NOW

Read 1 Corinthians 7:27-35.

> *Are you married? Do not seek a divorce. Are you unmarried? Do not look for a wife. But if you do marry, you have not sinned; and if a virgin marries she has not sinned. But those who marry will face many trouble in this life, and I want to spare you this.*
>
> *What I mean, brothers, is that the time is short. From now on those who have wives should live as if they had none; those who mourn, as if they did not; those who are happy, as if they were not; those who buy something, as if it were not theirs to keep; those who use the things of the world, as if not engrossed in them. For this world in its present form is passing away.*
>
> *I would like you to be free from concern. An unmarried man is concerned about the Lord's affairs – how he can please the Lord. But a married man is concerned about the affairs of this world – how he can please his wife – and his interests are divided. An unmarried woman or virgin is concerned about the Lord's affairs: Her aim is to be devoted to the Lord in both body and spirit. But a married woman is concerned about the affairs of this world – how she can please her husband. I am saying this for your own good, not to restrict you, but that you may live in a right way in undivided devotion to the Lord.* (1 Corinthians 7:27-35)

- What reasons does Paul give for some of the Corinthians to stay unmarried?
- Which of these were only relevant to the first century church?
- Why are the other reasons good ones for people choosing to be single today?
- Most single people have not made a conscious decision to be single for a lifetime but want to make the most of their singleness whether it is temporary or permanent. What are the practical implications of Paul's advice to those who would ideally be married?
- Paul remarks on the divided loyalties of those who are married. What do the married members of the group feel are the limitations on their Christian service? What advantages do they see for single Christians? Do the single people agree?

ACTION

- Review all that you have considered in these sessions. What are the major things you have learned?
- In what ways will your attitudes and actions be different?
- What actions could your church take to improve its appeal to single people?
- What can you do to implement needed change:
    - in the next week,
    - in the next year,
    - locally,
    - globally?
- How many of these activities can happen on their own initiative and how many require the agreement and active support of others or the whole church?

PRAYER

As you think back over the issues raised throughout the sessions, use the words of Psalm 23 (spoken over quiet music) to lead the group into a time of meditation and prayer.

The Lord is my shepherd, I shall not be in want.
He makes me lie down in green pastures,
he leads me beside quiet waters,
he restores my soul.
He guides me in paths of righteousness
for his name's sake.
Even though I walk through the valley of the shadow of death,
I will fear no evil, for you are with me;
your rod and your staff, they comfort me.
You prepare a table before me in the presence of my enemies.
You anoint my head with oil; my cup overflows.
Surely goodness and love will follow me all the days of my life,
and I will dwell in the house of the Lord for ever.

Booklist

Title	Author	Publisher
One of Us	Steve Chilcraft	Word Books
Single: The Jesus Model	Heather Wraight	Crossway Books
Suddenly Single: When a Partner Leaves	Phil Stanton	Kingsway
Out of the Blue: Responding Compassionately to Homosexuality	Martin Hallett	Hodder & Stoughton
Beyond Singleness	Helena Wilkinson	Marshall Pickering
Better Than, or Equal To?	Linda Harding	Word UK
Journey Through Single Parenting	Jill Worth, with Christine Tufnell	Hodder & Stoughton

Personal Profile:
SINGLE DIVIDE

After the vicar proclaimed David and Jane Newton husband and wife, it was another woman who divided that which God had joined together.

Married in 1986 within a year of meeting, they were both committed Christians, went to marriage preparation sessions and prayed long and hard over their decision to wed. But, six years later, David shunned God, Jane and their newborn baby, Daniel, leaving them all for another woman.

'I was sad the marriage didn't work out and will be sad about it for ever,' said Jane, who is now thirty-three. 'Looking back, I can't see any signs when we were engaged or before that which could have alerted me to what might happen.'

Self-discovery

Daniel is now five years old and lives with Jane, who works as a teacher. 'Because I have a beautiful son, I don't regret being married and I never will do. I love Daniel to bits and he's very secure in that – we have great fun too. I've learned to find out who I am again, what I enjoy, what makes me happy. It's a peaceful life, very straightforward and there's no conflict. I do miss the companionship of someone around the house, though. It's hard being single again and having to do everything: there's no one to share with. I never get a cup of tea in the morning and always go home to an empty bed.

At arm's length?

'My friends are kind, sympathetic and don't criticize me. After five years, they're surprised I've not met someone else. The fact I'm divorced is no big deal to them.'

But if only the same could be said about some of Jane's Christian acquaintances.

'The church I go to has an ethos of divorce being bad and I feel constantly a sense of my failure. Even to the extent that they warn people against having romantic involvement with divorced people. The clergy won't re-marry divorcees and that hurts – especially when they *will* marry non-Christians in church. I meet people and, sometimes, when they find out I'm divorced, they withdraw almost as if I'll contaminate their marriage. People who have known me from before the divorce remain good friends but even they don't like me talking about it, or even the good times of when I was married – they feel embarrassed, I think. There's a lack of understanding because they don't want to understand. What have I done wrong? I know I probably did – but David didn't say I'd done anything wrong. How can the secular world forgive but the church can't?'

Welcome support

Jane isn't totally without support, though. 'I still find it hard to trust other people but my relationship with God has taken off: without him my life is meaningless. I have to work hard at maintaining links with couples because they tend to forget I exist on Friday and Saturday evenings. I also have to plan ahead to ensure I don't have too many consecutive evenings on my own.

> '*I feel most supported when good friends welcome me into their home – not for anything special but simply to join in with what they're doing, to be part of their family.*'

'I feel most supported when good friends welcome me into their home – not for anything special but simply to join in with what they're doing, to be part of their family. What's particularly good is when I'm invited out and they arrange baby-sitting too! It's also nice when someone pops in for half an hour in the evening, it makes me feel cared for. When people ask me to help them out then that's also good because it makes me feel I have something of value to give to them. Two-way relationships are important.' And what about marriage? 'Half of me thinks no one would want to marry me and the other half that it would take someone very special. David and I were Christians when we married and it failed – what's to stop it failing again?'